Richard II

Graham Holderness was born in Leeds in 1947 and was educated at local schools. In 1965 he entered Jesus College, Oxford, gained a first in English and stayed on to take a B.Phil. in nineteenth-century literature. From 1970 to 1971 he worked as a Research Assistant at the Open University, lectured in English at the University College of Swansea from 1971 to 1982 and for the next five years was Staff Tutor in Literature and Drama at the Swansea Department of Adult Education. He is now Head of Drama at Roehampton Institute.

His publications include *D. H. Lawrence: History, Ideology and Fiction* (1982), *Shakespeare's History* (1985), *Wuthering Heights* (1985), *Women in Love* (1986), *Hamlet* (1987) and *The Taming of the Shrew* (1989). He has also edited *The Shakespeare Myth* (1988) and is co-author of *Shakespeare: The Play of History* (1988) and *Shakespeare: Out of Court* (1990). He is currently working on a Penguin critical study of *Romeo and Juliet* and editing a volume of essays on political theatre.

Penguin Critical Studies
Joint Advisory Editors:
Stephen Coote and Bryan Loughrey

William Shakespeare

Richard II

Graham Holderness

Penguin Books

For Rachel, Anna and Tess

PENGUIN BOOKS

Published by the Penguin Group
27 Wrights Lane, London W8 5TZ, England
Viking Penguin Inc., 40 West 23rd Street, New York, New York 10010, USA
Penguin Books Australia Ltd, Ringwood, Victoria, Australia
Penguin Books Canada Ltd, 2801 John Street, Markham, Ontario, Canada L3R 1B4
Penguin Books (NZ) Ltd, 182–190 Wairau Road, Auckland 10, New Zealand

Penguin Books Ltd, Registered Offices: Harmondsworth, Middlesex, England

First published 1989

Copyright © Graham Holderness, 1989
All rights reserved

Filmset in 9 pt Monophoto Times

Made and Printed in Great Britain by Richard Clay Ltd,
Bungay, Suffolk

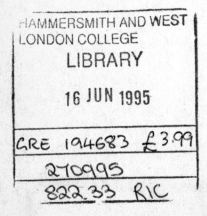

270995

Contents

Houses of York and Lancaster   vi

Introduction: History   1

1 King Richard   22

2 Bolingbroke   53

3 Minor Characters   68

4 Conclusions   89

   Further Reading   104

THE HOUSES OF YORK AND LANCASTER

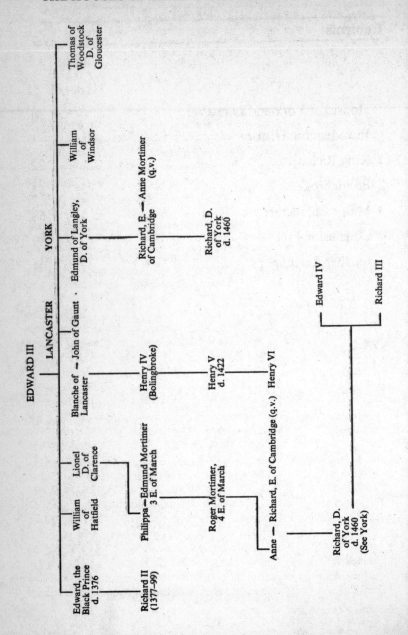

Introduction: History

History plays

Studying a 'history' play like *Richard II* presents certain problems which do not apply to the study of other types of Shakespeare play. Plays such as *Twelfth Night*, for example, or *Othello* or *The Tempest*, appear to be quite enclosed and self-sufficient, presenting the reader or audience with a complete, self-contained story. History plays like *Richard III*, *Henry V* or *Richard II*, however, each dramatize one small part of a much larger 'story': a great narrative of English history through the later Middle Ages into the Renaissance; an unfinished story, which was to the Elizabethans more familiar, if anything, than it is to us today.

As we read or watch a history play we are aware that episodes take place within the context of a larger action, and if we forget this the play itself will soon remind us. Events dramatized began before the play starts, and continue after its completion. The opening scene of *Richard II* is constantly referring back to events such as the death of Richard's uncle, Thomas of Woodstock, Duke of Gloucester, which belong in the past; and in the course of the play several characters (Richard, Bolingbroke, the Bishop of Carlisle) refer forward to events that fall outside the play into the unrealized vacuum of the future. This sense of 'incompleteness' presents us with difficulties and determines to some extent the methods we need to use in order to approach the play effectively.

The history, of which the play forms a small but important part, was well known to the Elizabethans: one of their standard history books, Edward Halle's *Union of the Two Noble and Illustrious Families of Lancaster and York* (1548), began at exactly the same point as Shakespeare's play, with the quarrel of Bolingbroke and Mowbray, which occurred in 1398. It was not to them, as we sometimes mistakenly imagine, a very recent history, continuous with and scarcely distinguishable from their own present. For Shakespeare to write in the mid-1590s about events that happened between 1398 and 1400 (the period covered by this play) was the equivalent of a modern playwright writing a drama about the French Revolution. But for the Elizabethans it was a very important history, since they regarded the period between 1400 and 1485, when the first Tudor monarch took the throne, as a time of upheaval and change

1

that ultimately created their own world – much as we might regard the late eighteenth century, with events like the French Revolution and the American War of Independence, as shaping the basic conditions of the modern world.

The later Middle Ages in England was a period of civil war, to which historians subsequently gave the name the Wars of the Roses. This long series of dynastic struggles between rival contenders for the throne, and their powerful families, ended only when Elizabeth I's own grandfather became King Henry VII. It was seen as a period of political unrest and social disturbance which gave way to an epoch of peace, social stability and national unity under the Tudors. At least this was how the history was shaped and interpreted in many of the historical studies that began to appear in the sixteenth century, among them Shakespeare's principal source for English history, Raphael Holinshed's *Chronicles of England, Scotland and Ireland* (1577, second edition 1587). These studies reflected an interest in history which certainly grew remarkably among the educated classes of Tudor England, and it was on the basis of such interest that a new historical drama could appear towards the end of the century on the first public stages. The historians also however reflected the interests of their ruling dynasty, the Tudors, and constructed, quite naturally, a version of history which cast the Tudor dynasty in the positive role of saviours of the nation, who brought lasting peace and harmony to a country wounded and weary after almost a century of bloody and disruptive civil war.

When plays about Richard III appeared in Elizabethan theatres in Shakespeare's time (and there were several of them) their dramatists were able to assume in their audiences an extensive and detailed knowledge of the whole of this historical narrative, which as we have seen was not only assembled and formulated, but *shaped* in a particular way by the historians before it ever reached the stage. The historical spaces that for us lie before and behind the dramatic text of a historical play, were for its original spectators alive and packed with well-known historical characters and events. We need to fill in some of those gaps if we are to understand what kind of 'history' a play like *Richard II* actually dramatized.

Elizabethan people didn't have to acquire and read rare and expensive printed books to obtained a knowledge of their history. History was alive all around them, in oral traditions, in legends, stories, ballads, songs and plays. The history of the civil wars I have been discussing could be seen and heard unfolding in public theatres where the basic price of admission was a penny.

I mentioned above two other history plays by Shakespeare, *Richard III* and *Henry V*. Both these plays form part of a large series of historical dramas written by Shakespeare (possibly, in the case of the earlier plays, with some collaboration from other writers), which when complete cover exactly the period from the deposition of Richard II (1399) to the death of Richard III at Bosworth, after which Henry VII became king (1485). The three parts of *Henry VI* and *Richard III*, though dealing with the later period, were actually written earlier than the 'second tetralogy' (*Richard II*, the two parts of *Henry IV*, and *Henry V*). Shakespeare was therefore going back in time when he turned to the subject of Richard II, and began to write that play with a consciousness of subsequent historical events.

There were plenty of different history plays by various authors also in production and circulation, and though there is little doubt that no dramatist other than Shakespeare attempted so ambitious a project as a huge mega-series covering the most important historical period known to the Elizabethans, his history plays would have interpenetrated with the other dramatic versions of history as well as with current prose and poetic historical narratives.

Family history

The older characters in the play are very conscious of the historical past. In I.2 the Duchess of Gloucester speaks to John of Gaunt (Duke of Lancaster) about 'Edward's seven sons' (I.2.11), and when Gaunt himself upbraids Richard on his deathbed, he refers back to Richard's 'grandsire' as a great king who would have denied the inheritance to Richard if he had been able to foresee the mess he would make of his kingdom. They are both talking about Edward III (ruled 1327–77), who is regarded throughout this play, as he was in Elizabethan historical tradition, as an ideal king, statesman and warrior. The Tudor monarchs were proud to trace their ancestry back to Edward III as a kind of fixed point of genealogical respectability. The eldest of Edward's seven sons, and therefore under the dynastic system of primogeniture (the eldest surviving son always inheriting) the first in line to the throne, was Edward the famous 'Black Prince', who in the event died before his father. Edward's fourth son was John of Gaunt; his fifth Edmund of Langley, the Duke of York in *Richard II*; his youngest Thomas of Woodstock, Duke of Gloucester, whose death is a central consideration of the play's opening scene.

The importance of this Plantagenet dynasty can be seen in the successive course of political history over the whole of the fifteenth century.

Richard, although only a boy when his father died, was none the less regarded by primogeniture as the true heir, since he was the eldest surviving son of the king's eldest son, the Black Prince, and so was crowned king in 1377. His surviving uncles, mature and powerful nobles like Lancaster (John of Gaunt), York (Edmund of Langley) and Gloucester (Thomas of Woodstock), any one of whom would obviously have made a more effective ruler than a child, acted as protectors of the realm during Richard's minority. Henry Bolingbroke, who after deposing Richard became King Henry IV, was the son of Edward III's fourth son, John of Gaunt. Henry's son and grandson inherited in direct line of descent, becoming Henry V and VI. When the latter was deposed in 1461, it was another branch of the same Plantagenet family that provided the 'pretenders' who were able to secure and hold the power of the crown for their family: Edmund Langley ('York' in the play) was grandfather to both Edward IV and Richard III. Looking at this dynastic history we can see that the Wars of the Roses were actually in one sense internal squabbles between members of the same family: all the major participants were descended from that one generation of brothers, the sons of Edward III.

This kind of dynastic history may well seem to us crustily antiquated and old-fashioned: perplexing to read, impossible to remember, and of dubious relevance to our modern sense of history, which is likely to take less interest in the internal power-struggles of royal families, and more in the lives of the millions of their 'subjects' whose social, economic and personal experience constituted the real history of the 'nation'. But a history play like *Richard II* is concerned almost exclusively with the intertwined personal and political destinies of that immensely powerful and influential royal and aristocratic family. The historical details noted above are alluded to or implied throughout the action of the play, and being aware or unaware of them is likely to influence the way in which we read and interpret the significance of the play's action.

When we see King Richard in the play's opening scene, presiding majestically over a complex legal proceeding, and holding all his subjects at a distance by an extreme formality of manner, it is important to remember that some of those subjects are his very close relatives. It would be easy to forget, as we hear Richard addressing the Duke of Lancaster as 'old John of Gaunt', and reminding him of his 'oath' of loyalty to the crown, that John of Gaunt is the king's uncle, who helped rule the kingdom during Richard's minority, and who might well under a different system of inheritance have been a contender for the throne himself (the historical Gaunt was certainly ambitious for a crown, and conducting numerous military campaigns in Europe succeeded in making himself 'King of Castile'). Of even greater significance is the fact that one of the 'appellants' in this trial, both of whom are apparently treated with scrupulous impartiality by the king, is not merely the king's cousin, but the son of Edward III's eldest surviving son, John of Gaunt. All this is pointed out quite explicitly in the text. Richard would not, he claims, favour Bolingbroke over Mowbray:

> Were he my brother – nay, my kingdom's heir –
> As he is but my father's brother's son . . .

> (I.1.116–7)

The very precise definition of Bolingbroke's family relationship to himself is clearly designed to minimize or conceal Bolingbroke's evident nearness to the throne. A dismissive phrase like 'my father's brother's son', with the addition of a qualifying 'but' (merely), makes Bolingbroke sound far less eminent than if he were to be described as 'son and heir to the Duke of Lancaster, eldest surviving son of Edward III'. In the same breath Richard talks of Bolingbroke's 'neighbour nearness to our sacred blood' (I.1.119), a remark which acknowledges the proximity of relationship his previous words sought to deny.

If everyone in this dramatized medieval society accepted the rules and conventions through which political power was transmitted and consolidated, then it would scarcely matter whether Bolingbroke were Richard's cousin, his brother, or an illegitimate son of one of his aunties: he would have no more right to challenge Richard's power, still less to depose and replace him as king. But if there is some possibility of disagreement about the legitimacy and authority of Richard's position, or if such doubt were called into being by serious discontent with Richard's kingship – if for example some of his powerful subjects were to query the rule of primogeniture, and question whether Richard's family descent really better equips him to be a king than Bolingbroke's – then there would be a much larger area of doubt within the play about the rights and wrongs of the historical process it describes. This is, as we shall see, exactly what does happen, so that considerations of family relationship remain very much to the fore and especially relevant throughout the political struggle and crisis dramatized by the play.

Later in this introductory chapter we will look more closely at the historical and historiographical contexts of *Richard II*: at the nature of the Elizabethan historical writing on which Shakespeare was able to draw, which we now know to be much more varied and diversified than appeared to earlier critics of the 'histories'; and at the various complex ways in which 'history' appears mediated and adapted to a specifically fictional and theatrical form within the play itself. In the meantime I will provide a summary of the main events of the play, setting them into the context of those preceding and subsequent historical events that constitute the large-scale historical process into which the play locates itself, and to which it continually alludes.

The action

Act I

SCENE 1
Richard II opens with a quarrel between two great nobles, the Duke of Norfolk (Thomas Mowbray) and Henry Bolingbroke, Duke of Hereford. Each accuses the other of high treason – that is, of some crime or misconduct prejudicial to the security of the state or the safety of the king. What exactly the quarrel is about we will need to look at in more detail. It involves a number of allegations, among them Bolingbroke's accusation that Mowbray conspired to murder his (and Richard's) uncle, the Duke of Gloucester. The important dramatic point of the conflict is that Richard is unable to reconcile the two contenders and is obliged to grant them an opportunity of trying their cause in a 'wager of battle' – the medieval process of law in which justice was supposed to be secured and guaranteed by the outcome of a fight, since whichever warrior was in the right would providentially be granted the victory.

SCENE 2
We then see John of Gaunt and the Duchess of Gloucester – widow of his murdered brother Thomas – debating the quarrel between Bolingbroke and Mowbray, and the king's part in it. It becomes evident from this scene that Gaunt believes Richard guilty of Gloucester's death (I.2.37–41). Both he and the Duchess seem to think that the combat has more to do with the killing of Gloucester than with anything else. The Duchess urges Gaunt to avenge her husband's death, presumably by taking up arms against the king. Gaunt refuses, arguing that Richard's sovereignty gives him immunity, and that only God has the right to apportion guilt and punishment.

SCENE 3
The combat scene presents the audience with a highly stylized and formal

historical ritual as the combatants prepare to fight. At the climactic moment Richard stops the combat and announces that he has decided the issue himself instead of leaving it to the result of a passage of arms. Mowbray is banished for the term of his life, Bolingbroke for ten years (which is then immediately commuted to six). Both barons are required to swear an oath that they will never conspire against the king. The scene closes with Bolingbroke taking leave of his father, who fears (correctly, in the event) that he will never see his son again.

SCENE 4

The next scene presents us with Richard in a more personal light and in a vein of rather more private conversation. Talking with one of his cousins and close supporters, Aumerle (son to the Duke of York, who will later be discovered conspiring against Henry IV), Richard discloses a fund of hostility towards Bolingbroke, suspecting him of treacherous ambitions (I.4.35–6). We also see the king deciding in a fairly casual fashion to 'farm the realm' (that is, to transfer portions of the royal revenues in exchange for sums of ready money – a kind of mortgage), and also to impose heavy taxes on the commons to finance a military campaign against rebellion in Ireland (I.4.42–52). Both these measures were historically entirely within the king's prerogative, and it was certainly his responsibility to levy armies to defend the realm. But these were also measures which proved unpopular and helped to fuel the discontent of the nobility and the gentry and small landowners with Richard's kingship. The scene ends with the news that John of Gaunt (Lancaster) is ill, and we see Richard praying that his illness might be terminal. This detail shows us that Richard already has plans to confiscate the Duke of Lancaster's property, which should by right of inheritance descend to his son Bolingbroke on his return from banishment. The play is a little vague on the details of this appropriation, but Shakespeare's historical sources are quite clear: as a banished subject Bolingbroke would not be able to take personal possession of his father's lands, revenues and title; but the king had granted him 'letters patent' (a written legal authority) to register his title in the courts should his father die during the term of the banishment. It would be up to the king to hold the property and manage it during Bolingbroke's absence, but it was obviously expected that the son would come into the inheritance on his return after six years. On Gaunt's death Richard actually revoked the letters patent granted to Bolingbroke (see II.1.202–4), effectively disinheriting Lancaster's heir.

Act II

SCENE 1

John of Gaunt's deathbed-scene is famous for his great patriotic celebration of England (II.1.40–50). Usually quoted as a description of an actual social condition, the speech in fact proves on closer inspection to be a nostalgic lament, addressed to his brother the Duke of York, for the absence in the England of 1398 of all those qualities for which Gaunt bestows on the country his patriotic love. It comes in the context of a long diatribe against Richard's rule, accusing him of being ruled by favourites, being a slave to fashion and heading for disaster. The England of Gaunt's memory ('this blessed plot') is now 'leased out' (II.1.59 – a reference to Richard's 'farming the realm') and 'bound in with shame' (II.1.63). When Richard enters with his court, Gaunt makes these accusations to his face. Richard reacts with defensive hostility, threatening that if Gaunt were not his uncle he would be in danger of execution.

When Gaunt dies, Richard immediately announces the seizure of his property. His uncle, York, remonstrates with him, pleading for the right of inheritance to be restored to his other nephew, Bolingbroke. The king ignores his petitions, and leaves for Ireland. The group of nobles left on stage – Northumberland, Ross and Willoughby – conduct a conversation which reveals a situation of considerable discontent with Richard's rule, and shows them giving serious consideration to the possibility of rebellion. They also accuse Richard of being led by flatterers; of being unsympathetic to the aristocracy; of taxing the people to excess; and of expropriating Bolingbroke. Northumberland reveals that Bolingbroke, supported by an army and by a group of dissident nobility, is already on his way to England.

SCENE 2

This scene extends the development of the previous one, providing a transition between Richard's temporary disappearance to Ireland, and the re-appearance of his great rival Bolingbroke in II.3. We first see Richard's Queen Isabel (in historical reality a child, in Shakespeare a young woman) suffering from an unfocused but prophetic melancholy, being comforted by Bushy. Richard's three aides – Bushy, Bagot and Green – here make one of their rare appearances. Systematically reviled as flatterers and upstart 'favourites' by Richard's enemies, two of them are later executed by Bolingbroke. When they appear in person, they seem curiously undeserving of the blackened characters bestowed on them by others. Here Bushy merely consoles the queen in her lord's absence; it seems to be stretching the evidence a little far to judge this as 'flattery'. Green brings news of Bolingbroke's return, and of the retinue of nobles who have joined his cause: the rebellion is under way. The appearance of York, nominated protector by Richard in his absence, confirms this as he describes his own loyalties as hopelessly divided between the one nephew, whose position as king he is both sworn and assigned to protect, and the other, whose fundamental social and political rights have been abused:

> Both are my kinsmen.
> T'one is my sovereign, whom both my oath
> And duty bids defend. T'other again
> Is my kinsman, whom the King hath wronged,
> Whom conscience and my kindred bids to right.

> > (II.2.111–15)

SCENE 3

The return of Bolingbroke is the signal for a scene devoted entirely to the aristocracy. Northumberland's obsequious courtship of Bolingbroke makes anything Richard's 'flatterers' say seem innocuous by comparison. Bolingbroke is introduced to Northumberland's son, Harry (Henry) Percy, who as 'Harry Hotspur' (see below) commands a substantial role in the next play of the series, *Henry IV, Part 1*. We observe Bolingbroke's forces augmented by the representative support of Ross and Willoughby, and then challenged by Lord Berkeley, a messenger from the regent York. York then appears in person to condemn Bolingbroke's return from banishment as 'gross rebellion and detested treason' (II.3.108). In an important statement (II.3.112–35) Bolingbroke argues that by denying his right to inherit his father's property and title, Richard has struck at the very root of the socio-economic system over which he presides. Richard is king, after all, only by virtue of an inheritance guaranteed and safeguarded by the generation of Bolingbroke's father. His arguments clearly act with powerful persuasiveness upon York, who is dislodged from his position as protector of the king's right into a dangerous neutrality which amounts in the end to complicity with the rebellion.

SCENE 4

Here we have another transitional episode, a choric scene of commentary on the action, typical of the dramatic rhythm of Renaissance tragedy. It is very short; it involves characters who play no great part in the drama (the Welsh Captain appears nowhere else in the play); and it conveys an important but simple piece of information – that Richard's military and political support is dissolving. But in the language of the scene we find a striking kind of poetry, initiated by the Welsh Captain, full of apocalyptic fear and prophetic anxiety. In his comparison of Richard to a 'shooting star' (II.4.19) Salisbury voices a mood and a poetry of tragic disaster which will became a keynote of the play.

Act III

SCENE 1

As Richard's power declines, so Bolingbroke's is seen to grow and consolidate. In a brief 'trial' Bolingbroke accuses Bushy and Green of misleading the king and injuring himself, and condemns them to death. The power he is arrogating by imposing death sentences on the king's supporters is of course enormous, and indicates already the scope of his ambition.

SCENE 2

Richard returns from Ireland, and greets his kingdom in a speech of curious tenderness and childlike fantasy. His supporters Carlisle and Aumerle urge him to adopt a more practical approach to the crisis, but Richard seems to rely on the metaphysical power of his own sovereignty: 'Not all the water in the rough rude sea / Can wash the balm off from an anointed king' (III.2.54–5). Salisbury brings news of the Welsh defection, and Richard is immediately plunged into a contradictory mood alternating abject despair and exaggerated confidence. A second messenger, Sir Stephen Scroop, brings a harsher tale of the kingdom's complete capitulation to Bolingbroke, and of the executions of Bushy and Green. Richard responds to this information with one of his great speeches of elegiac lament and tragic melancholy, and, despite the encouragement of his followers, seems ready to embrace defeat.

SCENE 3

The king has barricaded himself in Flint Castle, and Bolingbroke's forces appear close by. York is now with them, not with the king. At this point Bolingbroke insists that his purpose is no larger than to secure the repeal of his banishment, and the recovery of his expropriated lands and title. Richard appears on the castle walls, and attempts to subdue Bolingbroke and his followers with the powers of language and divine right. Northumberland plays a treacherous role as diplomatic mediator. The king seems to feel that concessions to Bolingbroke entail a complete renunciation of his authority; he himself is the first person to start talking about deposition (III.3.144). He comes down ('de-poses' himself) from the castle, entrusting himself to the rebels. Bolingbroke kneels in homage, but Richard appears convinced that his cousin's objective is nothing less than usurpation.

SCENE 4

The garden-scene is an interlude in the action. It tells us little that we don't already know, and serves rather to provide an opportunity for the dramatization of a melancholy queen's grief at her husband's dispossession, and for the emblematic political allegory of the Gardener and his assistants, who compare the management of a kingdom to the care of a garden. Bolingbroke seems to be proving a better gardener than Richard.

Act IV

SCENE 1

This, the only scene of Act IV, is the long deposition-scene which was apparently censored in its Elizabethan performances and in the earliest printed texts. Evidently the spectacle of a monarch voluntarily resigning the crown was thought to be matter too dangerous to be represented on the Elizabethan stage.

The scene opens with Bolingbroke, already acting as a king, holding a parliamentary meeting of the nobility. Its purpose is to investigate the Duke of Gloucester's death. Various accusations and counter-accusations are made by the nobles one against the other, each accompanied by a challenge to trial by battle. When the Bishop of Carlisle announces that Mowbray, Duke of Norfolk, is dead, Bolingbroke seems to regard the investigation as closed (IV.1.103–4). York then appears to tell Bolingbroke that Richard has agreed to adopt him as heir and to renounce his own claim to the throne. Bolingbroke becomes King Henry IV. The Bishop of Carlisle condemns the proceedings in a speech of powerful prophetic warning: the consequences of deposing a king will be dreadful civil war. Northumberland immediately gags the bishop by arresting him for high treason. Henry commands that Richard should be brought into public view, and seen to resign the crown voluntarily. Richard appears, and in a series of intriguing and powerful speeches makes abundantly plain that his resignation is forced and that he condemns his successor as a traitor and usurper. Richard is led away to imprisonment in the Tower of London. The scene ends with the Bishop of Carlisle, Aumerle and the Abbot of Westminster beginning to plot against Henry.

Act V

SCENE 1

Richard is led away, guarded, deposed and humiliated. Northumberland announces that the deposed king is to be imprisoned in Pontefract ('Pomfret') Castle rather than in the Tower. Richard foretells future divisions between Bolingbroke and Northumberland, between the usurper and his confederates; and of course in *Henry IV, Part 1* the Percy (Northumberland) family will be at war with the king. Richard takes leave of his grief-stricken queen.

SCENE 2

This scene indicates that resistance against the new king is already the order of the day. The Duke and Duchess of York describe Richard's departure from London. York's son Aumerle arrives, and York discovers his part in the Abbot of Westminster's conspiracy to murder Henry. York leaves to inform the king, followed by his wife and son.

SCENE 3

The new king is revealed already anxious about the career of another kind of rebel, his son Henry (later Henry V), whose career of apparent dissolution will occupy the two parts of *Henry IV*. The mention here of Prince Hal, who does not appear at all in *Richard II*, is one of the many clear indications that the larger historical series was already in preparation while this play was being written and performed. Aumerle (who has evidently ridden faster than his father) arrives to beg the king's forgiveness in advance of York's revelation. York follows immediately and urges the king to condemn his son as a traitor. The Duchess comes last, to plead forgiveness for her son. Bolingbroke puts an end to this strangely comic episode by pardoning Aumerle, and announcing that the other conspirators will be seized and executed.

SCENE 4

The shortest scene in the play and a miniature dramatic masterpiece, this brief episode shows Sir Piers of Exton, who is to murder Richard, interpreting and determining to execute Henry's unspoken desire: the death of Richard.

SCENE 5

Alone in prison, Richard soliloquizes on the mysteries and meanings of kingship, time, power, imagination. An anonymous Groom tells him the story of the former king's own horse accepting the new king as a rider. A Keeper then appears to command the Groom's departure. Richard acts with strangely uncharacteristic decisiveness and attacks the Keeper. In Holinshed's account Richard seized a pike from one of his eight murderers and killed four of them before he was subdued: this is the version used in, for example, the BBC / Time-Life Shakespeare Series dramatization. In the texts of Shakespeare's play there is no indication of the scale of his resistance apart from the Keeper's cries for help (V.5.104). Sir Piers of Exton immediately rushes in and dispatches the (former) king.

SCENE 6

The concluding scene strings together a series of episodes to confirm and then deny the security of Henry's power. Northumberland and Lord Fitzwalter in turn announce the executions of various enemies; Henry Percy brings news of the death of the Abbot of Westminster, and produces the Bishop of Carlisle for the king's judgment. Henry pardons the man who has conspired against him. By contrast he condemns the man who has acted on his behalf, as Sir Piers of Exton brings in the body of the murdered Richard. Exton receives neither reward nor favour. The play closes with Henry promising expiation for the guilt entailed in murdering a king.

Consequences

As I indicated earlier, it seems to me that we need to locate the internal action of the play into a larger external context of historical narrative, looking before and after. The latter operation is simple, since we have Shakespeare's own cycle of history plays to guide us. In the sequence of plays that dramatize English history from 1398 to 1485, from the deposition of Richard II to the accession of Henry VII, we can see that many of the details predicted in *Richard II* reappear or are fulfilled in those plays that deal with a later period; and indeed those 'sequel' plays frequently refer back to details in *Richard II*. Thus the civil wars predicted by the Bishop of Carlisle and by Richard certainly come to pass; attempts to depose the king and conspiracies against his life continue to haunt Henry, his son and the entire Plantagenet dynasty; Northumberland does come to regret having helped Henry, and his son Harry Percy has cause to remember Bolingbroke's courtesy with distaste; Henry IV's son Hal continues to give his father anxiety by his profligate and apparently un-princely behaviour; the myth of Richard as royal martyr continues to haunt his successors; and Henry IV continues to seek (and fails to find) absolution and peace of conscience for his part in Richard's murder.

But beyond these specific details of historical record, in the broad structural framework of the series as a whole we can discern the shape of a particular interpretation of history, which for many early and influential critics constituted the only context the history plays could possibly have had. The interpretation in question held that, since Richard II was a legitimate king (and indeed the last of the medieval kings to rule by undisputed hereditary right), to depose and murder him was an act of unnatural treachery and betrayal and a disturbance of the natural order of the kingdom and of the universe. This carried the inevitable fate of providential punishment to the criminal and to those who benefited from the crime. Thus the civil wars which divided England for almost a century were seen as divine retribution for original political sin. The reign of Henry IV was regarded as unhappy and troubled by these providential consequences; the punishment was briefly suspended during the glorious reign of Henry V, but renewed with a vengeance on Henry VI, whose reign saw the worst divisions of the civil war, and who was himself deposed and murdered. When the Yorkist branch of the family took power, the whole process of providentially inspired national disaster built up to a climax in the reign of the monstrous and deformed Richard III. With the aid of Providence Henry Tudor succeeded in slaying the Plantagenet dragon, restoring order to the troubled kingdom, and reuniting, by his own descent from John of Gaunt, and his marriage to the Yorkist heiress Elizabeth, the divided house of the long-suffering royal family.

Critics used to think this interpretation just about the only one avail-able to Elizabethan intellectuals, but the historiographical and scholarly work of the last two decades has shown that it was only one of several historical interpretations to be found embodied in Tudor history books. The principal ideological function of Tudor historiography was of course to affirm the legitimacy of the Tudor dynasty, so all the histories are quite clear that the accession of Henry VII was a 'good thing'. In their interpretation of the fall of Richard II, however, the Tudor perspective became more ambivalent. It could hardly be officially accepted in the 1590s that kings could be deposed by discontented subjects, and, as we have seen, the deposition-scene of *Richard II* was censored by Elizabeth I's civil servants. But the Tudors claimed their right to the crown through the Lancastrian rather than the Yorkist line, invoking Henry VII's descent from John of Gaunt. They tended to see the Yorkist kings (Edward IV and Richard III) as usurpers, though the Yorkist pretensions were to some degree appeased by Henry VII's marriage to Elizabeth, Edward IV's daughter. Inevitably their attitude to Richard was divided, since they wanted to vindicate the Lancastrian claim without defending usurpation. This ambivalent mixture of sympathy and distance is contained in Elizabeth I's embittered remark to her antiquary William Lambarde: 'I am Richard II,' she said (thinking of the treachery of the Earl of Essex), 'know ye not that?'

In the course of compiling their narrative accounts of the fourteenth and fifteenth centuries, the Tudor historians like Halle and Holinshed were drawing on sources which had been written and constructed from a variety of political and ideological perspectives. While the Lancastrian branch of the family held power between 1399 and 1461, in the persons of Henry IV, Henry V and Henry VI, there were chroniclers and historians doing exactly the same thing as the Tudor historians did: interpreting the past in ways favourable to the ruling dynasty. Thus among the historical materials available to Tudor intellectuals there were accounts expressing a Lancastrian version of the overthrow of Richard II: Richard was a weak and imprudent king, too easily led by time-serving and opportunistic flatterers, who lost the support of all sections of society by unjust, unpopular and even criminal acts of policy. The kingdom was so badly mismanaged that it became necessary to encourage Richard's resignation, which was given voluntarily, and to replace him with a new king who could command the support of the nation and rule the kingdom effectively. Bolingbroke's claim to the throne was supported by the powers of the aristocracy and ratified by parliament. Richard was not murdered, but died in captivity.

On the basis of this Lancastrian theory of history, there developed a powerful historical myth in which Richard was characterized as a tyrannical king, who tried to rule by his own will rather than by the common laws of the kingdom and the consent of the people. This myth can be found reflected within, for example, Holinshed's narrative. It also appears dramatized in some of Shakespeare's other sources, such as the anonymous play *Thomas of Woodstock* (c. 1594), where all the nobility are characterized as honest and patriotic Englishmen, while Richard appears as a tyrannical follower of Italian fashion and French political absolutism; or in the moralizing historical poem *The Mirror for Magistrates* (1587), where Richard is presented as a king who ruled 'all by blind lust'.

These anti-Ricardian accounts found their way into the Tudor chronicles, and there helped to bolster the claims of the Lancastrian inheritance.

So too did equally partial and biased pro-Ricardian accounts, such as a number of French chronicles, including the famous history of Sir John Froissart, and English accounts composed during the Yorkist rule (1461–1485), which presented Richard in a much more sympathetic light. The Yorkist interest was of course served by the depiction of the Lancastrians as usurpers, and of themselves as restorers of the line broken at the deposition of Richard. And the deposed king enjoyed much dynastic and political support in France. Despite the conflicts of the Hundred Years War, ties between the two kingdoms were still very close: Richard had actually been born in Bordeaux, and his second wife Isabel was a French princess. As a result French observers were much more inclined to see Bolingbroke as an unauthorized usurper and Richard as a martyr-king, an innocuous victim of illegitimate political violence.

It is possible that when Shakespeare was compiling material for a history play he may have worked in the same way as a historian, consulting a wide range of sources and comparing their different perspectives. He would not have needed to do this in order to find evidence of the conflict of historical opinion, since historians like Holinshed tended to amalgamate rather than synthesize their sources, letting diversified accounts stand side by side. Holinshed often uses the formula 'some writers say that ... while others offer a different view', without attempting to mediate or evaluate the correctness or authority of any one opinion. A careful reading of Holinshed's narrative alone would be enough to reveal that no single interpretation could really provide a final and definitive analysis of the history of Richard's fall.

Of larger importance than the question of whether Richard was viewed sympathetically or unsympathetically, is the broader consideration of how these different historical accounts interpreted and analysed the general significance of the history. The fall of Richard could be seen, as it was in the Yorkist myth, as an example of legitimate authority overthrown, with the consequence of serious divine displeasure; or it could be seen, as in the Lancastrian interpretation, as the overthrow of tyranny and the restoration of proper constitutional government. Since the Elizabethans tended to see historiography very much as a form of political education – from the successes and disasters of historical characters men could learn about the possibilities and constraints inherent in all political action – this difference of opinion raises the question of how the play could have been understood in its own immediate historical context. Most critics have assumed or argued that the play is royalist in sympathy: that it affirms, whatever faults Richard may have been guilty of, that a legitimate monarch rules by divine right and is protected by Providence, so that he cannot be deposed without severe punishment falling on the usurper. Interpreted in this way, the play would have functioned to endorse the authority of legitimate sovereignty. Ironically, however, the only evidence we have about how the play was received in its own time suggests exactly the opposite. On the eve of the Earl of Essex's abortive *coup d'état* of 1601, which attempted to overthrow Elizabeth, some of his supporters asked Shakespeare's acting company, the Lord Chamberlain's Men, to stage a performance of *Richard II*. They wanted to use the play as propaganda on behalf of the Earl's cause. So to them the play must have seemed to assert the rights of rebellion against tyranny, the legitimacy of deposing a bad monarch. In this reading of the play the hero was obviously Bolingbroke.

As I have already indicated above, Edward Halle, the most orthodox exponent of the Tudor historical myth, began his chronicle at the same point as Shakespeare began his play, with the quarrel of Bolingbroke and Mowbray. That choice of starting-point tends to work in favour of the Yorkist perspective, since we begin with a situation in which Richard's rule is given – an established fact – while the unrest and disorganizing conflict of the barons seems to offer a subversive challenge to the legitimate status quo. But as I have also indicated, the play doesn't take its own beginning as an absolute starting-point – it is continually alluding to events and actions of the past. And if we supply some details of the preceding history of Richard's reign, then we open up the possibilities for interpreting the general significance of the play's historical action.

Precedents

To regard the quarrel of Mowbray and Bolingbroke as the inception of a long and profoundly important historical process, as Halle did, is to cut it off, as an event, from the historical circumstances that produced it. In Holinshed's chronicle the quarrel is not a starting-point, but one stage in a long and complex series of political struggles. If we arrive at the quarrel in the course of reading Holinshed's long account of the earlier political events of Richard's reign, we may well take a different view of the significance of that conflict than the one offered by Halle. Let us look at some of the history which preceded the beginning of *Richard II*, as it was openly available to Shakespeare in his principal source, Holinshed.

We can enter Holinshed's narrative conveniently in 1386. In that year Richard advanced two of his close friends, Aubrey de Vere and Michael de la Pole, to high office – they became, respectively, Duke of Ireland

and Lord Chancellor. These men, like the 'favourites' depicted in *Richard II*, were not members of the old aristocratic families that formed part of the country's ruling élite, and did not have their support. A group of powerful nobles formed themselves into an organized opposition, and succeeded in securing the support of the Commons in a bid to have de la Pole accused of treason. The strategy employed here is of course a form of opposition against the king. But it belongs to a political situation in which it is very difficult, if not impossible, to confront or oppose the king directly (for reasons suggested by John of Gaunt in I.2).

Now this detail immediately offers us a different view of the Mowbray–Bolingbroke quarrel. It is quite clear from the play, and from the history, that Mowbray has acted for Richard, and is keeping quiet about the assassination of Gloucester on the king's behalf. It is equally clear that Bolingbroke's specific grievance is the murder of his uncle, of which the king himself is evidently guilty. But Bolingbroke does not accuse the king himself directly of that murder (which would of course be treason) but addresses the accusation obliquely to the king's supporter.

Despite the obstacles inhibiting the nobles, Holinshed tells that they succeeded in getting rid of the despised 'favourite', affirming parliament to be a sovereign body in the state, and assigning thirteen lords to 'have oversight under the king of the whole government of the realm'.

The political conflict between king and aristocracy addressed here is a deeply important one in English history, and raises all sorts of comparisons and echoes. Superficially it may have seemed at the time little more than a restoring of the custodial role the nobility enjoyed during Richard's minority: putting the king back on probation, as it were, until he could prove himself fit to rule. Yet this king was no child, and the power of his prerogative was sufficient to discourage any open attack on his person. In a longer view, it resembles earlier medieval struggles between king and nobility: the history of Edward II, for example, and more particularly, the establishing through Magna Charta of constitutional restraints upon King John. The interest such political topics held for the Elizabethan dramatists can be exemplified by Marlowe's dramatization of the tragedy of Edward II, and Shakespeare's own early history play about King John. With the advantage of hindsight, the situation even seems to prefigure the constitutional struggles between King Charles I and parliament, which also ended, a couple of decades after Shakespeare's death, in civil war and the execution of a king.

Holinshed reports that after the aristocratic successes of 1386, there were rumours of a plot between Richard and his supporters to quash what had by now taken shape as a baronial opposition and dispose of its leaders – the Duke of Gloucester and the Earls of Arundel, Warwick, Nottingham and Derby. This organized aristocratic opposition was led by Gloucester – the king's uncle, Thomas of Woodstock – and included among its leading protagonists both Mowbray (Nottingham) and Bolingbroke (Derby).

Richard's response to the events of 1386 was to pack a parliament with justices who were prepared to declare the proceedings of the previous parliament illegal and treasonable. The implications of such a judgment were of course very serious for the nobles, who resorted to armed struggle, and managed to inflict a defeat on the king's forces at the Battle of Radcot Bridge. The victorious army was led by Richard's 'father's brother's son', Henry Bolingbroke himself. Richard was besieged in the Tower of London. The lords continued to insist that they had no personal quarrel with the king, but had raised their powers to defend both king and realm against 'evil counsellers'. Yet they could in the same breath demand that Richard should leave the Tower and attend at Westminster, and that if he refused they would choose another king.

The baronial opposition was now in the driving seat. In the 'Wonderful Parliament' they declared the previous parliament illegal. The king's favourites were accused of treason by the five leading peers. Some of the king's men were banished, some executed. Richard was forced to swear an oath to abide by the rule of the aristocracy.

In 1397 Mowbray confided to Richard that the Duke of Gloucester and the Earls of Arundel, Warwick and Derby (Bolingbroke) were conspiring to assassinate the king. This is the point at which Mowbray changed sides, making the transition from a leading member of the opposition to being an associate of the king. Warwick and Arundel were arrested and indicted. Arundel was beheaded, Warwick exiled. The most dangerous opponent, the Duke of Gloucester, was imprisoned at Calais, and there, fearing to risk a public trial and execution, Richard had him secretly murdered. The entire leadership of the baronial opposition was thus reduced to one: Bolingbroke.

Having disposed of most of the opposition, Richard proceeded to govern as a tyrant. 'He began to rule,' says Holinshed, 'by will more than by reason, threatening death to each that obeid not his inordinate desires.' Richard used a neutered parliament to consolidate his power, taxing heavily, disinheriting estates, running up huge crown debts and requiring new oaths of allegiance from those said to have supported Gloucester's party (compare the complaints of the nobles in *Richard II*, II.1). As the king and the policies of the crown became increasingly unpopular, the people began to focus on the only surviving member of the baronial opposition. Putting this to strategic use for the last time, in 1398 Bolingbroke accused Thomas Mowbray of treason.

As we shall see in more detail when we come to discuss the play's textualization of history, to assume, as most critics writing on this play have assumed, that we can begin with Richard presiding over the quarrel of Bolingbroke and Mowbray, is to produce a limited interpretation of the play's 'history'. But if we know from Holinshed, and from the play's continual recursive glances back into its own pre-history, that this appeal of treason was not the beginning but the end of a long process of political struggle, in the course of which such accusations against a 'favourite' had frequently functioned as coded assaults against the power of the king, then surely we are likely to produce a quite different interpretation. Does it not make a considerable difference if we know (for example) that the king had been involved for several years in a protracted struggle with the nobles, which at one point came close to civil war; that Gloucester and Bolingbroke had been leaders of a powerful and persistent opposition, prepared to go to great lengths to secure their own interests and to curb the will of the king; that Woodstock's death was one of the measures taken by the king in dealing with a conspiracy against his own life; that Bolingbroke had led the army which inflicted on the king a humiliating defeat and landed him in the Tower? Consider what a difference it makes to our understanding of Mowbray's role if we are aware that it was he who betrayed the conspiracy of Gloucester and Bolingbroke to Richard.

At the heart of Holinshed's historical narrative – and, I will be arguing, at the heart of the play – is that long and tortuous struggle between the power of the monarchy and the power of the feudal nobility, which ended with victorious kings like Henry VII curbing the power of the aristocracy altogether, eliminating their military role in society and providing them with completely different administrative functions within the political and cultural apparatus of the state. No doubt this crucial weakness or instability was one of the factors that destroyed the feudal state: the king, ostensibly its central power, was actually its weakest point, strong only in his ability to control the powerful military leaders upon whose loyalty he depended. The ultimate success of later medieval monarchs in curbing aristocratic power proved to be one of the decisive distinctions between the medieval and modern worlds. It constituted an important part of that complex historical process that made Shakespeare's world a centralized Protestant Tudor nation-state, out of the European Catholic and feudal kingdom established at the Norman Conquest.

Influential critics like E. M. W. Tillyard tended to assume that Elizabethan political philosophy was largely moral and metaphysical in form, and innocent of the kind of interest in societies and political systems that we now call sociology. For the Elizabethans there was either order or there was disorder: the one was desirable, the other unthinkable. But it is increasingly obvious to us now that the Elizabethans had at their disposal at least the means for a much more sophisticated understanding of how other societies and different political systems operated.

It is my view that Shakespeare, together with many of his contemporaries, had some understanding of the sociological structure of a feudal society, which was perceived as radically discontinuous with, and different from, the English society of the 1590s. Certainly the historical imaginations of the Renaissance dramatists, particularly that of Shakespeare, dwelt on those turbulent centuries, the fourteenth and fifteenth, in which English feudalism experienced its death-throes, with striking determination and consistency of focus. It is my conviction that what they saw in that pre-history of their own present was not so very dissimilar from what modern historians have also seen there. To demonstrate that proposition of course involves more than awarding Shakespeare points for correctness of historical detail or persuasiveness of historical analysis. *Richard II* is a history *play*, and it is in the poetry and drama of its linguistic and theatrical medium that we must seek to identify the specific nature of its interest in, and its contribution to our understanding of, 'history'.

1. King Richard

The play opens with a note of authority: with a polite question which only lightly veils an authoritative command.

KING RICHARD
Old John of Gaunt, time-honoured Lancaster,
Hast thou according to thy oath and band
Brought hither Henry Hereford, thy bold son,
Here to make good the boisterous late appeal –
Which then our leisure would not let us hear –
Against the Duke of Norfolk, Thomas Mowbray?

(I.1.1–6)

If we wish to arrive at an accurate evaluation of the way in which Richard's 'character' is presented in the play, of the specific kind of 'kingship' his methods of government seem to represent, and also at an understanding of the kind of historical interpretation within which the play seems to frame him, we need to respond straight away to that tone of peremptory command. It has been very common, in both interpretation and performance of the play, for Richard to be represented as a weak, or passive, or effeminate, or dreamily impractical king. It seems to have been tempting and perhaps too easy for critics and stage interpreters to read back Richard's subsequent displays of weakness and despair, and to assume that the king, who later seems (at least to his followers) to give in all too easily, must have been characterized by endemic weaknesses of character from the outset. If we think of Richard as a man doomed to his ultimate defeat before the play begins, then we can easily miss the obvious strength and authority that are clearly visible in this opening scene.

If we assume that Richard is 'in reality' a weak and inadequate man, or a misguided and incompetent king, then we have to find some way of negotiating or explaining the confident dignity and serene majesty with which he presides over this critical situation. Critics who assume that this show of verbal strength masks weakness or corruption, argue that the very formality of Richard's language indicates an uncertainty, a lack of conviction, a hollowness in which can be detected the traces of personal weakness or the echoes of a guilty secret. Does Richard employ this ritualized artificial language to hide his weakness and guilt? Is his authority merely superficial, undermined by the moral infamy attaching to the murder of his uncle?

The first point to make is that the formal language and ritualized modes of address are of course appropriate to the situation. The confrontation of Bolingbroke and Mowbray is not even an ordinary state occasion or parliamentary council, either of which would in any case call for a measure of formality and decorum. Here Richard is presiding over a trial, a process of law which is, as we shall see, characteristically medieval rather than Elizabethan or modern; and he remains throughout very much in control of his 'court', presiding over the conduct of a difficult and complex legal process with apparent impartiality and a strict observance of procedure.

Several details of language in Richard's opening lines contain technical associations and levels of meaning which serve to emphasize the general air of legal propriety and correct procedure. When the king refers to John of Gaunt's 'oath and band [bond]', he invokes a very specific social relationship: the oath of fealty that binds the aristocratic subject in obedience to his lord. It was the father's legal obligation to be responsible for the good conduct of his son, and to ensure his presence at any legal hearing to which he might be summoned. The historical language tells us that this instance is not simply a case of the king's uncle doing him a family favour by collaring his refractory cousin. It is the much more complex case of one of the most powerful subjects in the realm being required on his oath of loyalty to perform for the king a service – bringing his son to trial – about which he might be (and later we discover he in fact is) understandably reluctant.

Bolingbroke has been summoned to 'make good the boisterous late appeal' which he has made against Thomas Mowbray. An 'appeal' was under medieval law an allegation, a criminal accusation which had to be formally made and formally heard by a presiding justice (here the king). The accused did not necessarily have to disprove the accusation in terms of what we could consider a legal process – presenting evidence, producing witnesses, cross-examination and so on. If the accused denied the charge, the dispute could go straight to trial by battle. As we shall see, this is exactly what Mowbray does, and trial by battle is decided upon as a consequence. The main point to establish here is that Richard's few opening remarks tell us a number of things: that this is a process of law, subject to strict rules of procedure; that the king is acting as the presiding judge; and that he is very much in control, scrupulously concerned to give both men a fair trial – 'impartial are our eyes and ears' (I.1.115).

One of the reasons why it is difficult to think of this opening scene as part of a 'trial' is that the legal processes involved belong to the period of the play's historical action, the later Middle Ages, rather than to the period of Shakespeare's time. In fact to an Elizabethan spectator the conduct of the trial must have appeared distinctly antiquated, not at all contemporary. The king asks Bolingbroke 'what dost thou object' (I.1.28) against Mowbray – what is the substance of his allegations. Bolingbroke's speech of reply (I.1.30–46), long and elaborate as it is, says only two things: Mowbray is a 'traitor', and he (Bolingbroke) is prepared to prove it so by force of arms – 'Thou art a traitor and a miscreant . . . What my tongue speaks my right-drawn sword may prove.' No 'proof' of a legal kind, no evidence, no witnesses, no statements: only the word of an aristocrat. But that is the nature of this kind of trial. Mowbray's reply (I.1.47–68) is even longer than Bolingbroke's speech of accusation, but again, it says only two things: Bolingbroke is a liar, and he (Mowbray) is prepared to fight him to prove it – '. . . I would allow him odds / And meet him . . . most falsely doth he lie'.

It is important to be fully aware of the sheer oddity of this procedure when looked at from the perspective of modern ideas about law and justice. We're all familiar enough with courtroom drama, if not with the dramas of the courtroom, to know that there is more to a trial than two people calling one another traitors and liars and then proposing a fight to decide who's telling the truth. But that is exactly the way in which the appeal of treason worked under medieval law. As a custom it belongs to a society in which the concept of 'loyalty' was profoundly important – the security of the kingdom could depend upon it – and one in which aristocratic notions of personal honour and family dignity gave a very special meaning to insults and allegations. An offence against the reputation of yourself or your family could be (as it still is with the modern Mafia, that descendant of the old aristocratic clan) a reason for killing. As far as Bolingbroke and Mowbray are concerned, once the accusation and denial have been made, there is only one other stage to this procedure: the challenge to battle. The two nobles dare one another to combat in chivalric language of an intensely antiquated kind:

BOLINGBROKE

  Pale, trembling coward, there I throw my gage . . .
  If guilty dread have left thee so much strength
  As to take up mine honour's pawn, then stoop.
  By that, and all the rites of knighthood else,
  Will I make good against thee, arm to arm . . .

MOWBRAY

    I take it up; and by that sword I swear
    Which gently laid my knighthood on my shoulder,
    I'll answer thee in any fair degree
    Or chivalrous design of knightly trial . . .

                                (I.1.69, 73–6, 77–81)

The king of course is presiding over this procedure, acting as an impartial judge. Yet the two aristocrats seem quite happy to arrange matters between themselves. Both Bolingbroke and Mowbray claim that their principal purpose is to defend the interests of the king and the state against an internal enemy: 'Tendering the precious safety of my prince' (Bolingbroke, 1.1.32); '. . . the fair reverence of your highness . . .' (Mowbray, 1.1.54). Yet both noblemen also explicitly separate their quarrel from the influence of the king: 'Setting aside his high blood's royalty / And let him be no kinsman to my liege' (Mowbray, 1.1.58–9); 'Disclaiming here the kindred of the King' (Bolingbroke, 1.1.70). Both claim to be acting in the interests of the king, and appealing to the king for justice; yet both are anxious to resolve the legal and political conflicts as quickly as possible in a single combat between two knights, where nothing will stand between them but their enmity and violence. When the two noblemen begin to speak that language of medieval chivalry, they seem between themselves to have more in common, despite their mutual hostility, than either has with the king. Chivalry is what unites them as well as being the chosen ground of their enmity.

Now in fact Richard does (and historically, did) hold a position of supreme power in this legal process. It is entirely up to him whether or not to permit the appellants to fight: they are obliged to seek his permission. As we see from the outcome of this trial, the wager of battle can be granted and yet stopped at any point by the king, who can then, if he wishes, give his own judgment – consulting, if it suits him, the members of his privy council (see I.3.118–24). Initially Richard does not exercise that supreme mastery, but he does not simply allow the knights to organize matters as they wish. He demands to know more of what Bolingbroke 'objects' against Mowbray:

KING RICHARD

    What doth our cousin lay to Mowbray's charge?

                                  (I.1.84)

Many readers have found Bolingbroke's charges against Mowbray vague and unconvincing. He accuses him first of all of embezzlement – fiddling the royal finances (I.1.88–91) – a charge which Mowbray easily answers

(I.1.126–132). Bolingbroke then elaborates on his initial charge of treachery by saying that Mowbray is not only a traitor but the biggest traitor in England, and leader of all the other traitors (I.1.92–7). Apparently in response to this, Mowbray openly admits (asking for a similar offence to be taken into consideration) that he once had criminal designs on Bolingbroke's father, John of Gaunt, but that this was an old quarrel long since patched up and the offender forgiven (I.1.134–142). This doesn't take us much further. Then suddenly, in the midst of all this vague and repetitive ritualized slanging, Bolingbroke makes an accusation that stands out with a startling clarity and simplicity:

BOLINGBROKE
> Further I say, and further will maintain
> Upon his bad life to make all this good,
> That he did plot the Duke of Gloucester's death,
> Suggest his soon-believing adversaries,
> And consequently, like a traitor coward,
> Sluiced out his innocent soul through streams of blood;
> Which blood, like sacrificing Abel's, cries
> Even from the tongueless caverns of the earth
> To me for justice and rough chastisement.
> And, by the glorious worth of my descent,
> This arm shall do it, or this life be spent.

(I.1.98–108)

Bolingbroke's language, usually flat and featureless or rather emptily rhetorical, here trembles and vibrates with a sudden access of intense emotion, issuing in a vigorous poetry of recrimination, expressing a passionate desire for justice. Gloucester's death is exactly delineated, and the haunting restlessness of his perturbed spirit vividly imagined. The feelings emerging from these lines with unmistakable clarity and strength are those of personal injury, personal grievance, and the powerful desire to exact and execute justice in one's own person, rather than leaving it to intermediaries or state officials. Bolingbroke might petition the king for 'justice' in the case, but 'rough chastisement' is the kind of vindictive punishment he himself desires to inflict on the putative murderer. Richard, though so careful to preserve his delicately balanced neutrality, permits himself here an ironic: 'How high a pitch his resolution soars!' (I.1.109).

Since Bolingbroke is talking to Richard about the violent death of their uncle, which both are well aware was commanded by the king and encompassed by Mowbray, it is evident that the thrust of Bolingbroke's challenge is now beginning to bypass Mowbray and is moving perilously close to targeting the king himself. The king's curiously prophetic comment – as if he already suspects that Bolingbroke's 'resolution' will soar as high as a claim to the throne – seems to indicate a full comprehension of these concealed implications. On this point Mowbray certainly is vague in his replies and in his defence:

MOWBRAY
              For Gloucester's death,
  I slew him not, but to my own disgrace
  Neglected my sworn duty in that case.

                                     (I.1.132–4)

Is that a confession of guilt, or not? What 'sworn duty' is Mowbray talking about – some unspecified undertaking made to Gloucester and broken by the murder? Or his duty to the king? Is he saying that he did not have Gloucester killed, even though the king ordered him to do so? Or is he merely referring to the reluctance which, according to Holinshed, kept the historical character Mowbray from despatching Gloucester for some three weeks after the king ordered his execution? The ambiguity of Mowbray's defence is of course understandable: since Gloucester was executed secretly, he can hardly admit openly to responsibility for an act of doubtful legality. Nor, having thrown in his lot so deeply with the king, can he openly implicate Richard. In fact for Mowbray the antiquated simplicity of a trial by battle must seem the clearest way of resolving a very tortuous position.

Mowbray concludes his self-defence by reiterating his innocence of Bolingbroke's charge of treachery, and his readiness to prove his honour in battle. It is at this point that Richard intervenes with a very important gesture of reconciliation, and attempts to make peace between the two combatants (I.1.152–9). Before considering the implications of that intervention, we need to take stock of what the scene has told us so far about Richard and about the nature of the political crisis with which he is confronted.

Clearly we have not so far in the dramatic narrative been given very much information of the kind we could define as 'character'. All the protagonists in this procedure are acting and speaking very much in their 'public' personae, uttering sonorous and declamatory speeches rather than confiding intimate details of personality. Richard is not acting here as a 'character', but as a king. The drama asks us to consider what kind of king he appears to be, and perhaps to assess his relative success or failure in dealing with a situation of conflict between prominent members of the aristocracy.

It is abundantly clear that the real issue underlying Bolingbroke's challenge to Mowbray is the death of Gloucester. This is endorsed by the subsequent scene, in which Gloucester's widow and her brother-in-law, John of Gaunt, make it apparent that as far as they are concerned the murder / execution of Gloucester is the key issue, if not the only issue at stake. The evident importance and centrality of Gloucester's death to the play presents certain problems, since the play itself does not provide any clear line on how that nobleman's death should be interpreted. The issue may have been left ambiguous because an Elizabethan audience would be expected to know the historical events surrounding the play, and to bring to their viewing of the play a clearly formed prior opinion. Given that Shakespeare evidently consulted a wide range of historiographical sources, which when placed together provide an extremely diversified and contradictory range of interpretations to explain Gloucester's death, it seems more likely that the issue was left ambivalent in order to disclose and highlight those contradictory historical interpretations that characterize the sources. Was the Duke of Gloucester a plain, well-meaning soul, brutally murdered by a machiavellian tyrant? Or was he an unscrupulous and determined political opponent, capable of plotting regicide, whom Richard was well-advised to get out of the way? Shakespeare's historical sources do not give any single or simple answer to that question. Does the play?

To most of the critics this scene appears to demonstrate Richard's inadequacies as a king. Here for example is the editor of the 'Arden Shakespeare' text of *Richard II*:

The first phase works towards, as its climax, a striking demonstration of Richard's unfitness for his kingly office. He has, first, the legacy of past mistakes to contend with. These mistakes are brought to dramatic life in the dead-and-gone business of Gloucester's murder, which has come alive again in the person of the avenging nephew and his challenge to the murderer's wretched tool, Mowbray; meantime, the Duchess of Gloucester, a lamenting chorus, serves to revivify for the audience the shock and horror, as well as the plangent dynastic issues, attendant upon the tyrant's buried act.

(Peter Ure, *The Arden Shakespeare: Richard II*, London, Methuen, 1956, p. lxiii)

This passage contains the basic components of many critical accounts of Shakespeare's play. The critic presupposes a Lancastrian view of Richard's kingship, based on the assumption of Richard's personal and political unfitness for royal authority. He deduces from the opening scenes the judgement that Richard can be described as a 'tyrant', and that the death of Gloucester was part of a haunting legacy of previous mistakes which return to plague the inventor. The audience, it is asserted, must necessarily share the Duchess of Gloucester's 'shock and horror' at the contemplation of Gloucester's brutal murder.

This seems to me the kind of interpretation likely to be offered when the play is read in isolation from its historical meaning and from the details of the history that surround it. For Peter Ure there can be only one understanding of Gloucester's death: that of the Duchess of York. Yet as we have seen, the historical conflicts of the later fourteenth century, which brought Gloucester into opposition with the king, are difficult to subsume into a simple black-and-white moralistic understanding of history. Richard's silence about the death of Gloucester can certainly be read as the repression of a crime by a guilty conscience. But the fact that the political group to which Gloucester belonged does actually succeed in overthrowing the king and placing a usurper on the throne, should surely indicate at least the possibility of Richard's having been (by the standards of the age) right, or at least well-advised, to get Gloucester out of the way.

A few other details in the play tend to endorse this recognition of the possibility that Gloucester may have been quite the reverse of an innocent victim. In the garden-scene, which provides a kind of choric commentary on the fortunes of Richard and Bolingbroke, the Gardener certainly suggests that Richard should have continued to take the toughest possible line with his opponents, cutting off the heads of 'too fast-growing sprays / That look too lofty in our commonwealth', as he cut off Gloucester's (3.4.34–5). Furthermore, we have the evidence of Gloucester's surviving brothers, Gaunt and York, who both obviously accepted, whatever their private feelings, the killing of their brother. York at one point despairingly wishes, 'I would to God – / *So my untruth had not provoked him to it* [my italics] – / The King had cut off my head with my brother's' (II.2.101–2). 'Untruth' means here 'disloyalty', a treacherous breach of faith. York feels that he'd like to have been executed, but he wouldn't want to have done what his brother did to deserve that fate.

If the play simply presented the various protagonists as individual characters, or as members of a particular family, then the kind of interpretation offered by Peter Ure would carry rather more weight; one doesn't, after all, make a habit of murdering one's uncles. But the actions and speeches of the characters, above all the kind of language they speak, are all saturated with detailed and elaborate historical meanings. Bolingbroke sees himself as engaged in a personal mission of revenge, an individual campaign to secure the restitution of justice. This is a stance he continues to affirm, even as he returns from banishment with an army and begins to occupy the country: 'My gracious lord,' he protests to Richard, 'I come but for mine own' (III.3.195). But, as we have seen from our survey of the play's pre-history, Bolingbroke's challenge to Mowbray can hardly be considered a private or individual matter. It is entirely consistent with the strategies of opposition engaged in by Bolingbroke, Gloucester and other members of the Lancastrian opposition throughout Richard's reign. What was always at stake in these political conflicts was power; and the kind of power wielded by Bolingbroke, here and later in the play, is very clearly the power of the aristocratic family historically pitted against the power of the monarch. If we criticize Richard later in the play for yielding to the pressure of unauthorized power, we ought at least in simple consistency to admire him for standing up against it at the outset.

Further misunderstanding of the play arises from a critical failure to appreciate the real significance of its chivalric language and of the medieval conventions and legal procedures presented in such elaborate detail. Many critics writing under the influence of E. M. W. Tillyard could associate political order only with monarchy: the 'formality' and decorum of the opening scene and the combat-scene could be seen only as the product of Richard's style of management.

The conspirators, working as such, do not share the ceremonial style used to represent Richard and his court . . . we have in fact the contrast not only of two characters but of two ways of life . . . the world of medieval refinement . . . is threatened and in the end superseded by the more familiar world of the present.
(E. M. W. Tillyard, *Shakespeare's History Plays*, London, Chatto & Windus, 1944, pp. 257–9)

The high formality . . . reflects a kingship which combines legitimacy with the assertion of a sanction ultimately divine . . . the legitimate but inadequate conception of feudal loyalty represented by Richard against the advance of a formidable but unsanctioned political energy.
(Derek Traversi, *Shakespeare from 'Richard II' to 'Henry V'*, London, Hollis & Carter, 1957, pp. 12–13).

Both these critics identify Richard's 'kingship' with a medieval 'order' overthrown by the unscrupulous political ambitions of a machiavellian 'new realism'. But as we have seen, although in theory Richard remains completely in control of the proceedings, the chivalric rules of the appeal of treason and the wager of battle give members of the aristocracy a kind of authority, a kind of power, that is independent of the power of the king, and can be turned against him. The cultural authority which gives

Bolingbroke the right to demand combat with his uncle's murderer derives from the codes and institutions of feudalism. Although the king presides over the proceedings, his control over their outcome is extremely tenuous, and if he grants the right to wager of battle – and lets the battle run its course – it is non-existent. Richard's position in the play symbolizes very precisely the predicament of a late-medieval king in a still largely feudal society.

The conflict which leads to the king's deposition is not a conflict between old and new, between medieval absolutism and modern power-politics. It is a conflict between the king's sovereignty, which he has been exercising in ways disapproved of by some of his most powerful subjects, and the ancient code of chivalry, which conferred all sorts of rights on the aristocratic subject. When Bolingbroke demands the right to chastise the murderer of Woodstock, he is demanding not what we would call 'justice', but individual revenge in reparation for personal insult and family dishonour.

Both Richard and Bolingbroke are therefore enacting particular kinds of policy, and the ideological conflict mapped by their antithetical policies constitutes a struggle for power within the later medieval state. When we see Richard offering to make peace between the antagonists, we should perceive something more than an ineffectual gesture backed by a poor joke:

KING RICHARD
Wrath-kindled gentlemen, be ruled by me:
Let's purge this choler without letting blood.
This we prescribe, though no physician;
Deep malice makes too deep incision.
Forget, forgive, conclude, and be agreed;
Our doctors say this is no month to bleed.

(I.1.152–7)

Richard's persuasive gesture, though ineffective, is hardly in its context an instance of crass incompetence. It is an attempt to substitute peace for hostility, forgiveness for enmity, and diplomatic conciliation for feudal violence. Of the two ideological positions here dramatized in contestation, the feudal and the monarchical, Richard's position is if anything the more 'modern' or progressive of the two. He is offering his warring barons exactly what Henry VII in 1485 offered the scarred aristocracy of the later fifteenth century: an opportunity to forget old scores and to reunite the divided realm in peace and friendship.

31

The failure of Richard's attempt at appeasement has less to do with his own capacities than with the stubborn and intractable adherence to feudal values of the protagonists themselves. Their refusal to accept the diplomatic overtures of Richard and Gaunt is again couched in the language of chivalry; for the two quarrelling dukes the issue has now resolved into an issue of personal and family honour.

MOWBRAY

> Myself I throw, dread sovereign, at thy foot.
> My life thou shalt command, but not my shame.
> The one my duty owes, but my fair name,
> Despite of death that lives upon my grave,
> To dark dishonour's use thou shalt not have.
> I am disgraced, impeached, and baffled here,
> Pierced to the soul with slander's venomed spear,
>
> . . .
>
> Mine honour is my life. Both grow in one.
> Take honour from me, and my life is done.

BOLINGBROKE

> O God defend my soul from such deep sin!
> Shall I seem crest-fallen in my father's sight?
> Or with pale beggar-fear impeach my height
> Before this outdared dastard? Ere my tongue
> Shall wound my honour with such feeble wrong,
> Or sound so base a parle, my teeth shall tear
> The slavish motive of recanting fear
> And spit it bleeding in his high disgrace
> Where shame doth harbour, even in Mowbray's face.

(I.1.165 71, 182 3, 187 95)

The number of technical terms that require footnoting (for example, 'baffled' – the rendering infamous of a recreant knight by public ridicule; 'parle' – a truce) give some indication of how thoroughly the dramatist has coloured his characters' language with an elaborate chivalric decor. The intensification of feudal language exemplified here is not to be found in any of the sources. Both opposition baron and king's man have broken away from royal authority completely and entered a separate realm of chivalric dedication and knightly honour. Each now cares more about his personal honour, which can be defended or demonstrated only by fighting, than about the ostensible cause of his coming to trial in the first place. The spirit of compromise activated by Richard, and endorsed by the loyal baron Gaunt, has failed to subdue the restless appetite for honour and action that characterizes the chivalric nobility. A monarchy aiming at a new kind of absolutist politics is crossed by the residual power of feudal institutions and ideology. Conceding a temporary defeat for his monarchical policy, Richard grants his subjects their trial by battle using their own language of chivalry and judicial combat:

KING RICHARD

> We were not born to sue, but to command;
> Which since we cannot do to make you friends,
> Be ready as your lives shall answer it
> At Coventry upon Saint Lambert's Day.
> There shall your swords and lances arbitrate
> The swelling difference of your settled hate.
> Since we cannot atone you, we shall see
> Justice design the victor's chivalry.

(I.1.196–203)

In fact of course when the day of combat arrives (I.3) we see nothing of the kind. Having granted the knights their day of destiny, and permitted the formal rituals of a tournament to build towards a breathtaking climax, Richard simply stops the combat and gives judgment on the issue himself.

In law, the king was entirely within his rights to do this, but legal authority is hardly sufficient to explain why Richard should choose such a moment and such a manner for something he could have done equally well at the very opening of the proceedings – by denying the knights right to battle, and judging the case himself. Why let things go so far? Is it a sudden decision, made in a moment of guilty panic? Or is Richard possessed by the fear that Bolingbroke might win, and the king's own complicity in Gloucester's murder thereby be revealed? Such explanations would appeal to those who see Richard as weak, indecisive and perpetually haunted by the guilt attaching to his uncle's murder. Or is it a deliberate, carefully planned and decisive intervention?

Let us consider the latter possibility. If the real political conflict here is between an aristocracy defending traditional feudal power and a monarch seeking to curtail the nobility and to arrogate greater authority to the crown – a king who is moving, in other words, towards the royal absolutism of the Tudor and Stuart monarchs – then the combat-scene shows us two things. Firstly it shows us the aristocratic class at the height of their power: resolving disputes and executing justice in their own way, simply by the exercise of their professional military skills, taking the issue quite out of the king's hands and rendering him temporarily powerless. But Richard's halting of the combat shows us a monarch determined to demonstrate the absoluteness of his personal power by overriding the preferences and privileges of the aristocracy, showing them who is master by the simple expedient of putting an abrupt stop to their little game. His intervention thus becomes an action undertaken not out of fear or panic, but from a determined will to demonstrate and impose supreme authority. If we try to explain this action in terms of Richard's inadequacies and weakness, we are likely to see the stopping of the combat as inexplicable, and to seek for concealed motives and hidden reasons. If on the other hand we recognize the historical context into which Shakespeare has carefully framed this political conflict, then the moment of the combat is precisely the right time to assert the royal authority and to openly and strictly suppress the disruptive feudal codes and customs that have brought it about.

All this is set forth clearly in Richard's speech of explanation: 'Draw near,' he commands the combatants:

KING RICHARD
> And list what with our council we have done.
> For that our kingdom's earth should not be soiled
> With that dear blood which it hath fosterèd,
> And for our eyes do hate the dire aspect
> Of civil wounds ploughed up with neighbours' sword,
> And for we think the eagle-wingèd pride
> Of sky-aspiring and ambitious thoughts
> With rival-hating envy set on you
> To wake our peace, which in our country's cradle
> Draws the sweet infant-breath of gentle sleep,
> Which so roused up with boisterous untuned drums,
> With harsh-resounding trumpets' dreadful bray,
> And grating shock of wrathful iron arms,
> Might from our quiet confines fright fair peace
> And make us wade even in our kindred's blood:
> Therefore we banish you our territories.

(I.3.123–139)

Richard has clearly proceeded with some caution here. He has consulted his privy council, thus making the judgment a collective rather than an autocratic one, and binding powerful magnates like Gaunt (who, as we see later in the scene, agreed with the judgment) to observe its implementation. Throughout the speech of proclamation there runs a powerful positive sense of what the kingdom might be if violent militaristic disruptions like the quarrel of Bolingbroke and Mowbray could be averted. The imagery Richard employs is that of pastoral poetry: he speaks of earth, and ploughing, and 'our fields', conjuring an impression of a tranquil, secluded and innocent countryside which would be violated by the harsh destructiveness of civil conflict – 'civil wounds ploughed up with neighbours' sword'. Parallel to the image of the quiet countryside is that of the sleeping infant, used to symbolize a fragile and vulnerable 'peace'; the child would be rudely awoken, the peace harshly disrupted by the dissonant sounds of battle. It is quite clear from Richard's decision to banish the combatants, and from the pastoral imagery employed in his speech of explanation, that he is proposing not simply to rid the country of a couple of trouble-makers, but rather to take a decisive stand against the disorganizing militaristic feudalism that threatens the security and tranquillity of the realm. If he can succeed in deporting the last remnants of his opposition, he will have moved some way towards dismantling the structures of feudal power.

Whether or not this is an admirable or desirable policy seems to me a matter of historical analysis rather than contemporary moral judgement. We certainly need to take a much more comprehensive view, and to take into account the perspective of the oppositional aristocracy, before we can arrive at any reasonably adequate summary of the play's attitude towards such matters. All I am concerned to establish at the moment is the arguable possibility that Richard's aspirations towards royal absolutism, in the given historical circumstances, might be considered legitimate and justifiable. He is certainly attempting to accomplish precisely what the Tudor monarchs succeeded in doing – disarming the aristocracy, 'gentling the nobility', depriving them of military power and incorporating them into a new kind of post-feudal state. His decision to take the dispute between Bolingbroke and Mowbray out of the hands of the aristocracy, to deprive them of their own codes of blood-feud and family honour and to insist on the matter being settled by 'parliamentary' discussion and agreement, parallels the persistent efforts of the Tudor government in Shakespeare's own time to stamp out duelling – that obdurate surviving remnant of the old institution of trial by battle.

The two scenes that follow, I.4 and II.1, show us a Richard relaxed from the severe formality governing his behaviour in the trial scenes. From the first lines of I.4, the tone is more naturalistic, more conversational, less ritualized, less schematic. 'We did observe' (I.4.1) – Richard enters in the middle of a conversation with Aumerle: he is no longer on public view, no longer assuming the ostentatiously dignified and impartial public persona of a king. In such a dialogue his more personal opinions and private feelings are likely to be revealed.

The formal respect, even affection, evident in Richard's previous addresses to Bolingbroke – 'cousin of Hereford' – gives way to a distinctly sarcastic and disrespectful tone: 'high Hereford' (I.4.2). Aumerle and the king speak of Bolingbroke with undisguised contempt and hostility. Despite the elaborate politeness of the previous scenes, it is clear that they regard Bolingbroke as an enemy:

KING RICHARD
  He is our cousin, cousin; but 'tis doubt,
  When time shall call him home from banishment,
  Whether our kinsman come to see his friends.

(I.4.20–2)

The remark is ambiguous. Will Bolingbroke on his return pay them a polite social visit (presumably a sarcastic inquiry)? Or is it more likely that those whom Bolingbroke returns to meet will no longer be regarded as 'friends'? Either way, the animus against Bolingbroke is unmistakable. In the remainder of that speech Richard elaborates on the grounds of his hostility, accusing Bolingbroke of courting the populace to curry political favour, and making it plain that in his view Bolingbroke has great political ambition. Bolingbroke acts:

KING RICHARD
  As were our England in reversion his,
  And he our subjects' next degree in hope.

(I.4.35–6)

He behaves, in other words, as if he expects the crown to 'revert' from Richard to himself, and regards himself as a principal contender for popular favour. We have already detected, in the underlying historical narrative, something of this latent political ambition, and we will see more of it when we come to examine Bolingbroke's actions and character in further detail. On the other hand it would be a mistake simply to accept Richard's model of an unquestionably legitimate authority – himself – challenged by a disorderly rebel.

The royal plural used in the phrase 'our England' paradoxically draws attention to the intensely personal quality of Richard's absolutist perspective: he regards England as his personal possession, not to be shared with anyone. It is this proprietary view of the nation, and Richard's unwillingness to provide within his social structure sufficient space for the expression and development of other people's hopes, fears, desires and ambitions, that proves more than any other factor to be his undoing. Many critics have seen this characteristically absolutist, imperialistic imagination as a distinctive feature of Richard's personality. I have been arguing that it should be seen, at least partly, in historical and political terms, as an enterprising though doomed attempt to resolve a particular set of historical contradictions. Both the psychological and the historical dimensions are present and interdependent in the play. It is, however, certainly true that as the action develops towards the denouement of Richard's downfall and deposition, the psychological dimension begins to come to the fore; though in my view it never eclipses the equally constitutive dimension of the historical.

As Richard makes plans for his military campaign against the Irish 'rebels', considering how his revenues can be increased by higher taxation, Bushy brings news of John of Gaunt's illness. Richard makes what is probably his most offensive remark in the course of the entire play.

KING RICHARD
> Now put it, God, in the physician's mind
> To help him to his grave immediately!
> The lining of his coffers shall make coats
> To deck our soldiers for these Irish wars.

(I.4.59–62)

Underlying this observation is of course the depth of Richard's enmity towards Bolingbroke and the Lancastrian 'party' in general, and we have already seen that such hostility is not without its justification. But the John of Gaunt we have seen in the play is a loyal and faithful servant of the crown, who has repressed his own misgivings and dissatisfactions in the service of his king. The casual and callous manner in which Richard wishes his own uncle, a distinguished elder statesman and loyal supporter, dead – simply in order to appropriate, by a piece of cheap opportunism, property for which he happens to have an immediate use – must surely deprive Richard of any sympathy he may have earned by his courageous resistance to a real historical threat.

The king's seizure of his subject's possessions is of course entirely consistent with that policy of absolutism with which Richard has attempted to check the encroaching impetus of baronial power. But it is surely also, considering Bolingbroke's character and popularity, a breathtakingly dangerous and imprudent gamble. In Richard's scheme of things there is no space for reciprocal agreements, for mutuality of interests, or for the equitable balancing of claims. If the crown has the power to take what it needs, it is the subject's obligation to give. Such a system will of course work only as long as the subject is prepared to acquiesce in political relationships which confer all power on the king, without requiring from him any reciprocal obligation towards the subject. Bolingbroke is not the kind of subject to endure such servitude for long.

The next scene, II.1., dramatizes a series of direct conflicts between the king and the nobility. The older generation of nobles, Richard's uncles, here appear less reluctant to challenge Richard's actions directly than the younger generation to which Bolingbroke belongs. We will examine in detail the specific arguments employed by Gaunt, York and Northumberland against Richard's character and style of kingship when we consider the function of the 'minor' characters. Our concern here is with Richard. Obviously stung by Gaunt's systematic diatribe of rebuke, Richard admits his ingrained hostility to the whole family. York asks the king to excuse Gaunt's forwardness:

YORK
  He loves you, on my life, and holds you dear
  As Harry, Duke of Hereford, were he here.

KING RICHARD
  Right, you say true. As Hereford's love, so his.
  As theirs, so mine; and all be as it is.

(II.1.143–7)

York objects to Richard's expropriation of the Lancastrian inheritance with an eloquent and compelling series of arguments about inheritance and tenure of property, which obviously represent the standard aristocratic view on such matters. Characteristically Richard does not wish to listen.

KING RICHARD
  Think what you will, we seize into our hands
  His plate, his goods, his money, and his lands.

(II.1.209–10)

'Think what you will': Richard speaks and acts with all the exaggerated and misplaced arrogance of an absolutist monarch confident of his supreme and unchallengeable power. He has no interest in the testimony of other voices, the contribution of other opinions, or the witness of other experiences, imagining that he can dispense with all these. York, who has hitherto, like Gaunt, been a loyal servant of the crown, will eventually join the rebellion and serve the new king. York is hardly (unlike Bolingbroke) a natural rebel, but the royal absolutism exercised by Richard seems to leave a man like York, with his ingrained commitment to the values of family, inheritance and private property, no political space in which to manoeuvre. The king's actions are such as to

YORK
   ... prick my tender patience to those thoughts
  Which honour and allegiance cannot think.

(II.1.207–8)

The most common way of reading the relationship between these scenes, where we see Richard in a relatively 'private' capacity, and the opening scenes, where his behaviour is completely public and formal, is to conclude that in the informality of private and 'family' conversation we see the reality of Richard's character and kingship, while the state occasions amount to elaborate pretences, artificially simulating a political order that actually masks anarchic tyranny. This view would be more persuasive if Richard's political perspective appeared substantially different in each case, but it does not. The contrast is much more a matter of tone and manner than of policy. Richard shows himself to be an absolutist monarch in the political, legal, cultural, economic and private spheres; there is no inconsistency. Whether we like or admire what we see of him is really a separate question, perhaps in some ways an irrelevant one. The alternatives posed in this play by history seem to be severely limited: an intractable choice between an absolutist monarchy or an aristocratic oligarchy. The latter force eventually overcomes, and places its own chosen leader on the throne. It remains to be seen whether or not the play presents this as an improvement.

Richard's departure for Ireland marks the beginning of the king's long absence from the play, during which period of time the return of Bolingbroke is anticipated, foretold, planned, unsuccessfully resisted and accomplished. Before we see Richard again, Bolingbroke will appear in a position of commanding authority, surrounded by a militant aristocracy now loyal to him, and ordering the execution of some of the king's leading supporters (III.1). Another scene (II.4) shows us the dissolution of the king's military support. In short, by the time Richard returns from Ireland, the ground has been carefully prepared to restore him to a pre-determined situation of defeat. Just as in the opening trial by battle, forces were arraigned but not permitted to meet, so for all the mustering of troops and mobilization of armies in Act II, there is no fighting. The king is to learn the consequences of ruling without popular support, or, more particularly, without the support of that belligerent warrior class which can if it wishes command more military strength than the king. The kingdom falls to Bolingbroke without a struggle, and Richard returns to find his reign effectively at an end.

This evaporation of concrete military and political support is an important determinant of Richard's dramatic role throughout the remainder of the play. For it is only in a situation where his 'kingship' – his title to the crown, the legitimacy of his authority to rule – becomes in a sense purely theoretical and symbolic, that he begins to invoke and appeal to supernatural powers and metaphysical aid. All Richard's famous observations about the divine right of kings appear in this middle section of the play:

KING RICHARD
    Not all the water in the rough rude sea
    Can wash the balm off from an anointed king.
    The breath of worldly men cannot depose
    The deputy elected by the Lord.
    For every man that Bolingbroke hath pressed
    To lift shrewd steel against our golden crown,
    God for his Richard hath in heavenly pay
    A glorious angel. Then if angels fight,
    Weak men must fall; for heaven still guards the right.

                                    (III.2.54–62)

KING RICHARD
    . . . we thought ourself thy lawful king.

                   . . .

    If we be not, show us the hand of God
    That hath dismissed us from our stewardship;
    For well we know no hand of blood and bone
    Can grip the sacred handle of our sceptre
    Unless he do profane, steal, or usurp.

                                (III.3.74, 77 81)

KING RICHARD
    Yet know, my master, God omnipotent,
    Is mustering in his clouds on our behalf
    Armies of pestilence; and they shall strike
    Your children yet unborn and unbegot,

That lift your vassal hands against my head
And threat the glory of my precious crown.

(III.3.85–90)

This is a very important and widely misunderstood dimension of the play. It is often assumed that the 'divine right of kings', the belief in a supernatural sanction authorizing the power of the monarchy, is one of the forces underpinning Richard's rule from the outset. The Tudor and Stuart monarchs of Shakespeare's own period certainly claimed such supernatural authority. But the idea was much more potent and widespread in that later period than it ever had been in the time of Richard II. Earlier medieval kings tended to govern more by social contract, sharing power with their nobility and clergy, than by claims to absolute power: if they could keep their barons on their side, they didn't actually need to claim the support of God as well. But it is widely believed that the Elizabethans did not have a modern sense of 'history'. It is thought that they imagined earlier periods of history very much in terms of their own contemporary ideologies and systems of belief. Thus when they dramatized the monarchies of the fourteenth and fifteenth centuries, they naturally assumed those earlier kings to have ruled under the same supernatural sanctions claimed by Elizabeth and by James I.

As I have already indicated above, this view seems to me quite mistaken. Much Tudor and Stuart historiography is quite the reverse of naïve and unsophisticated, and Shakespeare's historical plays always dramatize and imagine societies of the past in very specific sociological detail. The most significant feature of this play's presentation of the idea of divine right is that it begins to be affirmed by Richard only when all the concrete and material means by which a monarchy may be sustained have dissolved, leaving Richard in possession only of symbolic majesty. However powerful the myth of divine right may be, the play shows that a king *can* be deposed by the hands of men; the sacred balm *can* be washed off from an anointed king; God does *not* intervene in the crisis to avert Richard's downfall. The play shows Richard's kingdom to be in actuality a social contract, which, when not sustained by mutual trust and reciprocal obligation, becomes fragile and easily shattered. The powerful myth of divine right emerges from the break-up of that feudal contract, and then it is unable to heal the social breach from which it was generated.

On his first reappearance in III.2, Richard does not immediately affirm the political theory of divine right in its true historical form. The speech in which he embraces his kingdom with a peculiarly intimate patriotic tenderness actually seems to be a perversion of the doctrine of divine right. It moves from being a serious political philosophy of metaphysical kingship to a superstitious expression of primitive magic. The emotions expressed are oddly passive and quiescent, coming as they do from a king who knows that he will have to fight to have any chance of regaining his power.

Another way of putting this would be to say that Richard's feelings are strangely feminine; and in this play femininity is always associated, as we shall see when discussing the female characters, with weakness, passivity, impotence, frustration or failure of will. These characteristics are attributed to women and diametrically opposed to the traditional qualities of the aristocratic male, who is meant to be active, courageous, decisive, belligerent. In the course of that long exchange of accusation and defiance between Bolingbroke and Mowbray in the play's opening scene, Mowbray clearly distinguishes the kind of battle he wants to fight from the kind of conflict that might be engaged in by women.

MOWBRAY

Let not my cold words here accuse my zeal.
'Tis not the trial of a woman's war,
The bitter clamour of two eager tongues,
Can arbitrate this cause betwixt us twain.
The blood is hot that must be cooled for this.

(I.1.47–51)

It is hard to imagine a more precise or more decisive definition of an absolute and irreconcilable difference between the sexes. Fighting, an active and positive enterprise, is done with the 'blood' and body, and it can only be done by men. The only kind of fighting Mowbray can imagine women engaged in is a scolding squabble between 'two eager tongues'. The energy and vigour that characterize masculine militarism are absent from the latter activity: the woman's words are 'cold', while the warrior's blood is 'hot'. There is even a latent accusation of constitutional cowardice on the part of women, who are far more 'eager' to engage in the cold clamour of a verbal quarrel than they would be to undertake the physical challenge of a real battle. The patent substance of Mowbray's words is of course an accusation against Bolingbroke, tantamount to a charge of effeminacy. He (Mowbray) is too manly to join in this humiliating conflict of words, and cannot wait to get on to the field where the real 'trial' can begin.

In III.2 Richard, at precisely the moment when he needs the strength and purposive determination of a soldier and a leader – virtues which in the play are the prerogative of the male sex – seems possessed by those opposite qualities attributed by feudal and chivalric ideology to the female gender. Richard 'weep[s] for joy' when reunited with the 'dear earth' of his kingdom; and he compares his relation to his realm to that of a mother to her child:

KING RICHARD
    As a long-parted mother with her child
    Plays fondly with her tears and smiles in meeting,
    So weeping, smiling, greet I thee, my earth,
    And do thee favours with my royal hands.

                                                    (III.2.8–11)

There could be no stronger contrast than that between Richard's behaviour in this scene and Bolingbroke's in the preceding scene (III.1), which dramatizes the 'show trial' of Bushy and Green. Bolingbroke's cold anger and peremptory authority express not simply a difference of character, but contrasting kinds of patriotism and very different conceptions of how one relates to one's 'country'. Bolingbroke's repossession of his estates, which prefigure his subsequent claim on the kingdom as a whole, is enacted with an ostentatious display of legal formality, a formidably rational explication of causes and motives, and a coldly self-possessed conviction of righteousness. Richard by contrast displays an intensely personal and subjective relationship with his 'England', cherishing the land with an almost sentimental tenderness. Where Bolingbroke reclaims his property with legal argument and military duress, Richard exercises his fantasy to populate the realm with an imaginary host of familiar spirits, and then conjures them to resist the rebel occupation. The divine right of kings is reduced to a primitive superstition, or rather to the kind of fantasy we might meet in a child who invokes the power of imaginary familiar creatures to combat the apparent omnipotence of parents.

KING RICHARD
    Feed not thy sovereign's foe, my gentle earth,
    Nor with thy sweets comfort his ravenous sense,
    But let thy spiders that suck up thy venom,
    And heavy-gaited toads, lie in their way,
    Doing annoyance to the treacherous feet
    Which with usurping steps do trample thee.
    Yield stinging nettles to mine enemies;
    And when they from thy bosom pluck a flower
    Guard it, I pray thee, with a lurking adder,
    Whose double tongue may with a mortal touch
    Throw death upon thy sovereign's enemies.

                                                    (III.2.12–22)

There is something palpably absurd about this attempt to fight a battle for possession of a kingdom with an army of spiders, toads and stinging-nettles, mustered in a childish anthropomorphic fantasy. Indeed an 'internal stage-direction' (a point in the text where stage action or business are called for by something one of the characters says) informs us that this speech should be played to provoke an effect of absurdity. Richard's companions, Aumerle and the Bishop of Carlisle, appear to be laughing at the king's antics:

KING RICHARD
  Mock not my senseless conjuration, lords.

                                       (III.2.23)

What Richard is doing here is separating the kinds of power he can claim by gestures of language and acts of the imagination – divine right, hereditary title, legitimate authority – from the more practical and concrete powers of military support, strong defence and adequate security. The observations of Richard's followers indicate how dangerous is this splitting of effective from symbolic power.

BISHOP OF CARLISLE
  Fear not, my lord, that power that made you king
  Hath power to keep you king in spite of all.
  The means that heavens yield must be embraced
  And not neglected; else heaven would,
  And we will not – heaven's offer we refuse,
  The proffered means of succour and redress.

                                    (III.2.27–32)

The Bishop of Carlisle, who can be expected to speak with some authority on such matters, makes it abundantly clear that the divine power which legitimates Richard's authority will not operate automatically and without the active co-operation of human agency. Where Richard looks for an army of angels (backed by a reserve force of spiders, toads and stinging-nettles), Carlisle's strategy would be to provide God with the biggest army he could find, and then let divine power take its course.

Richard's response to his pragmatic advisers is to reject outright the force of their arguments, declaring them irrelevant; and here his language reaches a level of abstraction where fantasy is no longer obstructed by uncomfortable facts. Confronted with a real material challenge, Richard can only identify himself with those symbolic properties that dominate the discourse of divine monarchy. In that discourse the king is compared to the sun ('*le roi soleil*'): incomparably bright, pivotal, life-giving. So Richard comes to believe that he *is* the sun: he imagines his personal majesty as possessing the power of the sun to eliminate the guilty shades of darkness.

KING RICHARD
So when this thief, this traitor Bolingbroke,

. . .

Shall see us rising in our throne, the east,
His treasons will sit blushing in his face,
Not able to endure the sight of day . . .

(III.2.47, 50–3)

Rapt by his own solipsistic fantasy, Richard seems unable any longer to distinguish symbol from referent – 'see us rising in our throne, the east' – or to preserve any sense of the distance between a metaphor and the reality to which it alludes.

The inverse side of this megalomaniac hubris is the vertiginous collapse into despair which now becomes Richard's characteristic response to adversity. At one moment overweeningly confident, at the next plummeting into abject desolation, the king rides a dizzying see-saw of contradictory extremes, unchecked and unmodified by the palpable pressure of reality.

KING RICHARD
All souls that will be safe fly from my side,
For time hath set a blot upon my pride.

AUMERLE
Comfort, my liege. Remember who you are.

RICHARD
I had forgot myself. Am I not King?
Awake, thou coward majesty; thou sleepest.

(III.2.80–4)

Hearing of the defection of his supporters and the deaths of Bushy and Green, Richard swings abruptly from the exaggerated extremity of his conviction of divine right, to the melodramatic intensity of his vision of 'the hollow crown':

KING RICHARD
             Of comfort no man speak.
Let's talk of graves, of worms, and epitaphs;

. . .

> Our lands, our lives, and all are Bolingbroke's,
> And nothing can we call our own but death
> And that small model of the barren earth
> Which serves as paste and cover to our bones.
> For God's sake let us sit upon the ground
> And tell sad stories of the death of kings –
> How some have been deposed, some slain in war,
>
> . . .
>
> All murdered. For within the hollow crown
> That rounds the mortal temples of a king
> Keeps death his court; and there the antic sits,
> Scoffing his state and grinning at his pomp,
> Allowing him a breath, a little scene,
> To monarchize, be feared, and kill with looks,
> Infusing him with self and vain conceit,
> As if this flesh which walls about our life
> Were brass impregnable; and humoured thus,
> Comes at the last, and with a little pin
> Bores through his castle wall, and – farewell, king!
> Cover your heads, and mock not flesh and blood
> With solemn reverence. Throw away respect,
> Tradition, form, and ceremonious duty;
> For you have but mistook me all this while.
> I live with bread, like you; feel want,
> Taste grief, need friends. Subjected thus,
> How can you say to me I am a king?

(III.2.144–5, 151–7, 160–77)

Richard's despair is in a sense the divine right of kings inverted, turned inside out. The king who surrounded himself with elaborate fantasies of divine and magical sympathy was imagining himself alone, isolated from humankind, communing only with supernatural beings. But here Richard realizes the dreadful truth that symbolic majesty is not in practice separable from political power. If he has lost the latter, then the former will automatically evaporate from him and be conferred upon another. The great figure of symbolic kingship which dominated Richard's imaginative universe, occupying the heavens in isolated splendour and sun-like majesty, suddenly becomes a lonely man, for the first time aware of his human vulnerability. Tradition, form, ceremonious duty, are all conventional gestures that can be 'thrown away': the sovereignty they symbolize does not after all inhere in the person of the king, but only in the impersonal institution of monarchy.

A deposed king possesses less than nothing. Not only are his property and even his life forfeit to the victorious usurper, but the loss of a quality of 'royalty', which the king has always conceived as an element of his own personality, also entails a loss of fundamental and constitutive identity. A man who has been a king from earliest childhood can't hope to return to being plain Richard Plantagenet. Everything he has been is gone, and what he now is, 'subjected' to another king, seems impossible and unbearable. All Richard can now possess is that capacity to die which those in despair often paradoxically conceive of as the last affirmation of existence. The prospect of death is not simply an escape from an intolerable reality; it can also be an active assertion of individual integrity, the means by which a 'subjected' individual can positively extricate himself from the power of others.

If Bolingbroke possesses his 'life' and his 'land', at least Richard can arrogate his own 'death', and occupy a property that no-one else could covet or share, the grave. That grotesque image of the grave as a kind of pie-crust, 'modelled' in earth and covering the decomposing corpse, establishes a pattern of imagery which is then sustained and developed throughout the whole speech. The dominant motif could be defined as 'hollowness'; and the images are all of outer coverings lightly or barely containing some hidden emptiness or corruption within. The hollow grave covers the bones of the dead with a fragile 'paste' of earth; the 'hollow crown', which appears to protect and secure the body of the king, in reality contains an empty space echoing with the sardonic mockery of the 'antic' – death; the 'flesh' or human body, which 'walls about our life' like a defensive 'castle wall', appears to be as strong as 'brass impregnable' – but in fact it can be breached with an instrument as weak and innocuous as a 'little pin', and inside it is nothing but an isolated and vulnerable life, easily extinguished. All these images derive from Richard's new-found awareness of human vulnerability, as his life is touched by those forces of adversity from which he believed himself to be immune. But he has attained such an intensive realization of that vulnerability through the experience of discovering the apparent security of divine majesty to be, once it has been emptied of its real content of effective political and military power, a hollow shell.

It is not of course entirely accurate to say that Richard possesses nothing except the power to die. He also stands possessed of a profoundly imaginative awareness of the transience of power and the emptiness of metaphysical kingship, which amounts to a potent myth of royal tragedy.

He may have no material possessions, no property in the realm that might be inherited by his heirs, but what he can bequeath to his successors is in some ways larger and more permanent than property: his own tragic myth.

KING RICHARD
> For God's sake let us sit upon the ground
> And tell sad stories of the death of kings . . .

(III.2.155–6)

Richard has already started on the construction of another compelling story, which he will transmit to future generations, to be told and re-told many times. We are in a sense now re-telling it over again: Shakespeare's play *Richard II* represents another recital from that same mythography, another sad story of the death of a king.

It is important to observe that what we see here in the play is a story in the process of construction; what we witness is the means by which the story is initiated and framed. The play does not simply represent the tale of Richard's martyrdom as a reality that came into being through certain historical circumstances. Rather it demonstrates the specific conditions from which Richard's myth of royal martyrdom was composed as a narrative structure; and in particular it reveals the key role of Richard's own agency in fostering its composition. It may seem a fine distinction, but it is a profoundly significant one.

I have said that Richard begins to grasp at alternative kinds of power only when the effective political authority on which he has relied begins to dissipate, and I have defined that process as the strategy of an imagination facing defeat. From another point of view, the alternative sources of power on which the king begins to draw – poetry, myth, self-dramatization – though unlikely to win any battles, are certainly effective means of getting your point of view included and retained on the historical agenda. We would not now be considering the dramatized experience of Richard's fall if these ideological powers had not proved in some ways more potent than the big battalions that actually won the war.

From here to the very end of the play Richard continues to alternate between a kind of philosophical resignation, in which he constructs fantasies of escape and retreat, retirement and reclusion, and a kind of inspired imaginative resistance, through which he challenges his oppressors not on the level of military or political contestation, but rather on the 'aesthetic' level of persuasive moral commentary and potently emotional self-dramatization. At certain moments his strongest impulse

is towards self-abnegation by means of resignation, retirement, the re-
clusive life of a hermit or wandering pilgrim, piously longing for an
anonymous death:

KING RICHARD
>What must the King do now? Must he submit?
>The King shall do it. Must he be deposed?
>The King shall be contented. Must he lose
>The name of king? A God's name, let it go.
>I'll give my jewels for a set of beads,
>My gorgeous palace for a hermitage,
>My gay apparel for an almsman's gown,
>My figured goblets for a dish of wood,
>My sceptre for a palmer's walking-staff,
>My subjects for a pair of carvèd saints,
>And my large kingdom for a little grave,
>A little, little grave, an obscure grave . . .

(III.3.143–54)

At other points in the protracted process of his downfall, he places
himself not on those romantic margins of society towards which his
pastoral fantasies lure him, but right at the very centre of the court,
where he claims and holds a kind of attention capable of throwing
everyone else – including the taciturn and self-effacing Bolingbroke –
into the shadows. The best example of this latter strategic gesture in
Richard's campaign of 'fantasy resistance' is the deposition scene,
IV.1.

When Richard offers to 'submit' and to accept deposition, he is
taken at his word. York announces to a full parliament, presided over
by Bolingbroke, that Richard is prepared to 'yield' his sceptre to his
cousin: in other words, to abdicate. The purpose of the ensuing scene
for Bolingbroke and his supporters is to stage-manage a public display
of that abdication, designed to convince all observers of the legitimacy
of their own proceedings. They hope to show Richard has resigned his
crown voluntarily; to demonstrate Richard's unfitness for office by
forcing him to confess to a list of 'crimes'; and to prove Bolingbroke's title to the crown legitimate – authorized by Richard's
voluntary resignation and by his willing adoption of Bolingbroke as his
successor.

The entire procedure, obviously devised and stage-managed by Bolingbroke and Northumberland (and perhaps York, who certainly plays
a prominent formal role in what follows), is designed to function as a
ritual of legitimation:

BOLINGBROKE
  Fetch hither Richard, that in common view
  He may surrender. So we shall proceed
  Without suspicion.

(IV.1.155–7)

In the event Richard turns the occasion into a very different kind of
ritual, clearly demonstrating the illegitimacy of Bolingbroke's coup, and
his own unwillingness to resign. By means of a series of elaborate ritual
displays, Richard shows that his resignation is forced rather than voluntary: that the process enacted is a deposition, not an abdication.

  Richard begins immediately on his entry (IV.1.162) with a speech that
makes play with the contradictions inherent in a transfer of kingly power.
Can the attributes of sacred majesty, and all those qualities of dignity
and authority that make a king the recipient of service, loyalty, even
worship, simply be conveyed to another person, another body, by legal
formula or parliamentary proclamation? And if the powers of divine
right really are in some way located within the person of the king, then
those who depose him are guilty of a betrayal comparable to the treachery of Judas, who betrayed Christ.

RICHARD
                I hardly yet have learned
  To insinuate, flatter, bow, and bend my knee.
  Give sorrow leave awhile to tutor me
  To this submission. Yet I well remember
  The favours of these men. Were they not mine?
  Did they not sometime cry 'All hail!' to me?
  So Judas did to Christ. But He in twelve
  Found truth in all but one; I, in twelve thousand, none.

(IV.1.164–71)

By comparing himself to Christ, Richard is not only claiming a supreme
metaphysical status and authority, he is also anticipating his own martyrdom. Like Christ, he clearly does not expect to repossess an earthly
kingdom; he expects to be murdered. But he is also preparing, like
Christ, to leave behind on his departure from this world a powerful
myth of divinity violated and innocence slaughtered. When asked to
make a public display of his resignation, Richard doesn't exactly refuse
to do so. Nor does he play the role prescribed for him by his captors,
obediently submitting to, and thereby legitimating, their authority. He
makes the transfer of the 'crown' into his own chosen ritual (181–99),
using the physical object, the crown itself, as a prop in a dramatized

tableau of unwilling deposition. He obliges Bolingbroke to hold the crown with him as he hands it over, and thus incorporates the reluctant usurper into a ritual display expressing the deposed king's grief, disappointment and sense of injustice. In place of the smooth and unproblematical transfer of power intended by Bolingbroke, the exchanging of the crown comes to mean something quite different: not 'this is the voluntary resignation of a kingdom', but 'this is the spectacle of a usurper unjustly seizing the crown from an unwilling but defeated monarch'. Bolingbroke is forced into a repetition of questions which raise doubts, anxieties, qualifications – 'I thought you had been willing to resign' (IV.1.189), 'Are you contented to resign the crown?' (IV.1.199) – and thereby interrupt and disturb the planned simplicity and clarity of the ritual of 'abdication'.

Richard's next symbolic gesture is a detailed and formal inversion of those rituals employed to confer power and authority on a king – rituals of coronation and investiture. Richard publically 'un-kings' himself, literally and metaphorically removes from himself all the ceremonial signs of majesty, 'undoing' all the rites by means of which a king's authority is vested in his person. He removes the crown, gives up the sceptre, symbolically washes away the 'balm' which anointed him, renounces his 'pride of kingly sway' and his 'sacred state', releases his subjects from their oaths of loyalty, forgoes all his property and revenues, and cancels his laws. By means of this symbolic anti-coronation, Richard insists on every detail of his deposition being observed and understood, refusing to permit any aspect of the process by which power is stripped from him to remain unnoticed.

The next stage in Bolingbroke's pre-arranged programme of events is that Richard should be obliged to confess to a charge-sheet of allegations prepared for him by his accusers: one of the standard ingredients of a 'show trial'. Richard refuses to do this, and turns the accusations of criminal behaviour against the usurpers, again claiming a symbolic companionship with Christ: '. . . you Pilates / Have here delivered me to my sour cross . . .' (4.1.239–40).

By declining to make the prescribed confession, Richard is refusing to authorize Bolingbroke's succession. Though he has no power to prevent or oppose his rise to power, he has the capacity to cast over Bolingbroke's kingship the guilty shadows of treachery, usurpation and (in anticipation of the expected martyrdom) regicide.

Finally, in the ceremony of the mirror (IV.1.264–90), Richard again reverts to his earlier observations about the deceptiveness of appearances. By breaking the glass, so shattering the image of his own face, he simultaneously demonstrates the vulnerable fragility of kingship, and anticipates his own assassination.

Richard's last appearances reveal him alone, in prison. In a sense this solitary confinement is the culmination of Richard's absolutism. A prison is a world without people, a kingdom without subjects, an empty space which can be filled with Richard's own personality, dominated by his own unobstructed, undeflected will. Here Richard can imaginatively populate his own kingdom by playing, in fantasy, many parts. None of the characters he plays are 'contented', all unhappy, but that scarcely matters: if the entire kingdom has taken on the colour of Richard's sorrow, then his domination of state and people is, at last, secured.

2. Bolingbroke

If, as I have argued, Richard's 'character' – however individual and idiosyncratic it may be – is inseparable from the political actions and historical circumstances through which that character is expressed and changed, then the same observation is certainly true of his 'mighty opposite' (to use a phrase from *Hamlet*) Henry Bolingbroke. In fact one very persuasive and influential critical view of Bolingbroke is that he is much more of a 'politician' than Richard, his personality correspondingly more 'subdued to what it works in', more easily defined in terms of the political actions he undertakes and the political processes he lives through. A critical distinction arises from that difference of character and approach: between the man who is perfectly adapted to the impersonal and manipulative business of politics, and the man who is constitutionally ill-adapted, the king who is more of a dreamer, or a poet, or an actor than a politician. But, as we have seen in discussing the relationships between the 'character' of Richard and the historical conditions within which his personality is realized, no fundamental or absolute distinction between 'character' and 'society' (or 'history' or 'politics') can be wholly satisfactory. Richard is as much a politician as Bolingbroke: only the policies he espouses and defends are different and diametrically opposed policies.

This view of Bolingbroke as a 'vile politician' (to use Henry Percy's damning phrase from *Henry IV, Part 1*) is deployed to explain why Bolingbroke's 'character' seems strangely one-dimensional compared with Richard's. Where Richard is enormously articulate and self-revealing, Bolingbroke is taciturn and self-effacing: Richard calls him at one point a 'silent King' (IV.1.289). When Richard loses power he becomes more eloquent, more verbose, assumes a more commanding stage presence: when Bolingbroke temporarily loses his (when he is banished) he simply disappears from view, and re-materializes only when he has gathered sufficient military support to provide himself with a substantial political presence.

Clearly it makes sense to a certain degree to think of Bolingbroke as very much a political animal. The motives he expounds to explain and justify his actions are always political motives; all his actions are directed towards the resolution of some political problem or the achievement of some political goal. The critical problem arises when we ask, since we cannot imagine a human being whose existence can be defined absolutely in terms of his or her external and objective behaviour, what actually lies 'inside' Bolingbroke's being. What are the emotional and psychological springs of Bolingbroke's actions; what residuum of feeling and conscious-ness lies at the bottom of his political rhetoric and his political success?

Now it seems to me that to formulate the problem in this way is to start off on the wrong track altogether. Such questions, and the critical problem they are addressed to resolve, assume some fundamental distinc-tion or even opposition between what is individual, personal or private in human experience, and what is collective, public or political. In this kind of ideological framework of ideas the 'personal' is always regarded as the essential or authentic stuff of human experience, and the public or political are conceived as a secondary realm of inauthentic behaviour and belief. Inspired by this critical assumption that the truly deep sub-stance of the play rests in its representation of character, a reader in search of Bolingbroke's 'soul' would have to conclude – in the absence of almost any really personal revelation – that Bolingbroke is driven by universal appetites such as ambition, or a hunger for power. Sooner or later this argument pushes us to raise the question: does Bolingbroke from the very outset consciously, actively and positively seek to obtain the crown?

Let us for a moment pursue this line of inquiry and see where it takes us, and let us in pursuit of it return to the opening scene. On the surface Bolingbroke seems to be quite open about his motives for challenging Mowbray. He regards the existence of a traitor in such close proximity to the king as a danger to the person of the king and to the security of the realm:

BOLINGBROKE
In the devotion of a subject's love,
Tendering the precious safety of my prince . . .

(I.1.31 2)

The motive is familiar, and it is expressed in such a way as to glorify the king and to endorse his power, while simultaneously attacking one who is in some way close to him.

BOLINGBROKE
Since the more fair and crystal is the sky,
The uglier seem the clouds that in it fly.

(I.1.41–2)

But of course, as we have seen, such a formulation was an easily recognizable code, an indirect way of attacking the king himself, whose supreme prerogative made it unthinkable for a subject to attack him directly. Bolingbroke's literal expressions are straightforward enough; his metaphors are susceptible of more than one reading. If the fair and crystal sky is Richard and the ugly clouds Mowbray and other unworthy or treacherous flatterers, then the metaphorical meaning is quite in keeping with the literal expressions of loyalty (to the king) and aggression (to Mowbray). But as in the sub-text of Bolingbroke's speech his hostility to Richard himself becomes clearer (though never openly expressed), another possibility arises. Perhaps Bolingbroke means to symbolize the monarchy itself, or the nation, by the image of the sky, and the king is one of the ugly clouds which disfigure and besmirch England's hereditary brightness.

Subsequent developments make it quite clear, as we have seen, that Bolingbroke's assault is in truth directed against the king, who is generally regarded as the instigator of Gloucester's murder. 'Real' or 'genuine' motives seem then to lie somewhere beneath the surface of a character's language and overt self-expression. Bolingbroke says he is acting in Richard's best interests, yet in reality he is opposing his power. What then are the hidden grounds of opposition?

In that prefatory speech the carefully modulated balance between respect for the king and contempt for his enemy is nicely preserved: Bolingbroke is almost punctiliously polite to Richard – 'so please my sovereign' (I.1.45). When angered by Mowbray's defiance, that poised equilibrium slips, and the accents of personal anger and resentment start to vibrate through Bolingbroke's language. In addition to the chivalric principles he shares with Mowbray, Bolingbroke also voices his scorn and contempt for Mowbray by alluding to his own 'royalty': he speaks of 'the glorious worth of my descent' (I.1.107) and of 'my high blood's royalty' (I.1.71). Deploying such phrases to assert his own elevated status, Bolingbroke claims a personal responsibility for punishing the murder of Gloucester – whose blood cries out 'to *me* for justice' (I.1.106; my italics) – and thereby elevates himself to the same level as the supreme justice, the king. In the combat-scene Bolingbroke impeaches Mowbray as:

BOLINGBROKE
. . . a traitor foul and dangerous
To God of heaven, King Richard *and to me* . . .

(I.3.40, my italics)

In what sense can Mowbray be described as a 'traitor' to Bolingbroke himself? Surely the kind of treachery being discussed here means an offence against the king or the state, not an injury to a private individual? But Bolingbroke regards an act that damages himself as a crime of equivalent magnitude, seriousness and gravity to an offence against God or the king.

In the light of our search for Bolingbroke's 'private' motives, the conclusion to draw from this is obvious: that Bolingbroke sees himself as possessing qualities of 'royalty', inherited properties of dignity and rank, which befit him as a candidate or contender for the throne. From the very outset we can see him pitting himself against the power of the king, and defining by his use of self-glorifying terms the full extent of his ambitions. The relation between 'personal' motive and 'political' action is in the terms of this argument entirely clear: Bolingbroke is driven by a generalized desire for power or worldly ambition, and is prepared to dissimulate, deceive and manipulate to gain his political ends.

The principal objection to this argument is that it supposes the 'real' meaning of the play to reside somewhere beneath or beyond the significance which appears on the surface of its language. We can hardly object to this as a method, since it is in a sense what critics do all the time; and some of the most important developments in modern ('post-structuralist') criticism have erected that 'absence' of meaning from language into a theoretical principle. But the kind of traditional critical interpretation I am talking about is guilty of two things. In its search for the 'real' meaning of a play, in character or subjectivity, and in its unwillingness to acknowledge the political as a serious domain of authentic human experience, it constantly misreads the intricate and complex interweaving of public and private, political and personal, that we find everywhere in Shakespeare's drama. And it tends to fill any apparent vacuum of meaning, any silence or open question in the text, with very contemporary prejudices and ideological predispositions – such as the ideological assumption that the individual subject is the only vehicle of authentic human experience, or the disillusioned modern intellectual's belief that 'politics' can never be anything other than a shabby and opportunistic deployment of dirty tricks and machiavellian manipulations.

Although one can certainly find in Shakespeare's plays an abundance of cynical and contemptuous references to the practice of politics, that fact should not be taken to imply that the plays adopt or express a merely hostile attitude to such practices. As I have already suggested, it seems to me that plays like *Richard II* display a much more engaged and curious interest in matters historical and political than we are likely to find in the jaded cynicism of the modern Anglo-American critic. That proto-sociological analysis of earlier civilizations – Rome, Athens, feudal Scotland, later-medieval England – was certainly within the capacity of an Elizabethan dramatist with a serious interest in history, and with sufficient intellectual curiosity to prompt a consultation of a wide range of historical sources.

The historiographical character of *Richard II* seems to me to be plainly visible on the surface of its language; and a recognition of its presence should encourage us to take seriously what Bolingbroke actually says, rather than disregarding his speeches as mere camouflage for thinly concealed political ambitions. To read Bolingbroke's language is to gain access to a personality in which political motives and principles rank very high and loom very large. But, as we shall see, in his character those political impulses are felt and experienced with an immediacy and intensity that make them indistinguishable from the deepest 'personal' needs and desires. Bolingbroke's loves and hates, his desire and anger, his pride and humiliation belong both to him and to the historical world of which he is an inseparable and irreducible part.

Let us look again at those details from the opening scenes which seem to suggest that Bolingbroke has designs on the throne from the outset, and that his 'political' statements are merely lies or half-truths calculated to cover his real motivations and designs. In the context of this subjective and ahistorical approach, Bolingbroke appears to be launching a full-scale assault against the king's authority, and offering his own credentials of 'royalty' and 'glorious . . . descent' to qualify himself for the job of king. But this is to asssume, as many critics do, that 'royalty' was a quality that could be possessed only by the monarch, as was the case with the absolutist monarchies of the Renaissance, where the king / queen was isolated within his / her ambience of divine majesty and didn't share power with anyone else. In fact in the world of *Richard II* people talk about 'royalty' and inherited status in quite a different way: terms that are more appropriate to the post-feudal kingdom which the historical Richard II actually governed, than to the Britain of Elizabeth I or James I. Richard in the play is claiming the kind of supreme personal power later possessed by the Tudor and Stuart kings. But the people around him, particularly the other members of his own family, tend to see majesty, authority and power as bound up with the aristocratic family itself rather than with any individual member of it. The Duchess of Gloucester defines this conception clearly, in a speech (addressed to John of Gaunt) which makes much play with the central and immensely significant image of 'blood':

DUCHESS OF GLOUCESTER
    Finds brotherhood in thee no sharper spur?
    Hath love in thy old blood no living fire?
    Edward's seven sons, whereof thyself art one,
    Were as seven vials of his sacred blood,
    Or seven fair branches springing from one root.

(I.2.9–13)

The image of the 'family tree' (which would be literally represented as a tree in old genealogical charts), together with the associated image of Edward III's 'sacred blood' (I.2.12), represents the family itself as a significant and sacred unit. All the brothers and their sons share that same blood: all therefore derive from their relationship to Edward a quality of majesty. In this 'kinship' theory of society authority is not vested in the king alone, but dispersed through the important (that is, male!) members of the family.

No crime could be greater or more unforgivable within this kinship system than the murder of a kinsman. The killing of Gloucester is conceived here as an offence against the family, a stain on the reputation of the aristocratic clan. Gloucester was a branch of the royal tree, a vessel of the royal blood, a participant and sharer in the dignity and power of Edward's sovereign line:

DUCHESS OF GLOUCESTER
    But Thomas, my dear lord, my life, my Gloucester,
    One vial full of Edward's sacred blood,
    One flourishing branch of his most royal root,
    Is cracked, and all the precious liquor spilt;
    Is hacked down, and his summer leaves all faded,
    By envy's hand, and murder's bloody axe.

(I.2.16–21)

The Duchess's insistent urging on of Gaunt to take revenge on his brother's murderers invokes a central principle of the same kinship system: the obligation that falls on members of a family to revenge their murdered kin. Since, as the Duchess observes to Gaunt, 'his blood was thine', it befalls to the brother to take revenge. Gaunt acknowledges this claim of blood, and the moral responsibility that goes with it.

JOHN OF GAUNT
    Alas, the part I had in Woodstock's blood
    Doth more solicit me than your exclaims
    To stir against the butchers of his life.

(I.2.1 3)

To return to Bolingbroke: if he, together with the other members of his family, shares this notion of collective majesty, and believes, as they all believe, that the particular individual member of the family who happens to be king ought to rule very much as a member of the family, incorporating his relatives into the machinery of the state and preserving their best interests, then his allusions to 'the glorious worth' of his 'descent' need not signify a candidature for kingship. If the supreme political body in the state is not the king but the royal family, then obviously an offence against that family can be conceived of as an act of 'treason' – which would normally be a term reserved for an injury to the person or dignity of the king himself. What has happened here of course is that the act of 'treason' – the murder of Gloucester – has been committed by the king. Those nobles like Gaunt and York, who are prepared to put up with (though they do not approve of or agree with) Richard's absolutist policy, believe that the king's guilty participation in that murder short-circuits the judicial system and makes it impossible for anyone to seek redress – the king has a right to execute subjects adjudged to be guilty of treason against himself, and no subject has the right to judge his king. Bolingbroke adopts the different, 'oppositional' view that if the king has committed 'treason' against the royal family, then the members of that family are obliged to proceed against him. In the combat-scene he formally requests from his father a statement of moral support – and gets it.

BOLINGBROKE
> Oh thou, the earthly author of my blood,
> Whose youthful spirit in me regenerate
> Doth with a two-fold vigour lift me up
> To reach at victory above my head,
> Add proof unto mine armour with thy prayers . . .

JOHN OF GAUNT
> God in thy good cause make thee prosperous!
> Be swift like lightning in the execution,
> And let thy blows, doubly redoubled,
> Fall like amazing thunder on the casque
> Of thy adverse pernicious enemy!
> Rouse up thy youthful blood, be valiant, and live.

(I.3.69–73, 78–83)

Bolingbroke appeals to that same quality of 'blood' which has been used to define the dignity and status of the royal family. In his use of the blood-image, he is both glorifying his father's military exploits (later the Duke of York recalls to Bolingbroke the occasion when he and Gaunt 'Rescued the Black Prince – that young Mars of men – / From forth the ranks of many thousand French', II.3.100–101) and linking those who share both the royal blood and his own consciousness of injury into a party, united in feeling, if not in policy, against the king. Gaunt, for all his strict sense of loyalty to the crown, evidently sees no contradiction in wishing his son the victory, and metaphorically bestows on him the god-like power to execute justice by thunder and lightning. It is the blood of Edward III ('rouse up thy youthful blood') that will achieve victory, revealing Mowbray's guilt and striking a significant blow against the authority of the king. Shakespeare's John of Gaunt, who is often thought of as a patriotic apologist for absolute monarchy, is actually (as we shall see in discussing his character in more detail) a defender of the old feudal oligarchy – king and aristocracy bound together by bonds of reciprocal obligation ('fealty') into a powerful and irresistible ruling class. At this point Gaunt makes it plain, by speaking the language of blood, kin and vengeance recently uttered by the widowed Duchess of Gloucester, that his sympathies lie with the injured family rather than with the legitimate but 'treacherous' (in Bolingbroke's sense) king; with the old feudal contract rather than with the new royal absolutism being developed and asserted by Richard.

A comparable exchange between Bolingbroke and his father occurs after Richard has stopped the combat and pronounced the sentences of banishment. Bolingbroke has very little to say to the king, but his words are carefully weighed and ambiguously significant:

BOLINGBROKE
> Your will be done. This must my comfort be:
> That sun that warms you here shall shine on me,
> And those his golden beams to you here lent
> Shall point on me, and gild my banishment.

(I.3.144–7)

This ingenious play on words asks first of all to be read as a kind of regretful compliment. In Elizabethan political thought the sun was a symbol of majesty; in the later stages of the play Richard is frequently compared to the rising or the setting sun. Bolingbroke has done what he could to protect and preserve 'the precious safety of [his] prince', and has been unjustly maligned and punished. His only 'comfort' is that wherever in the world he may go, he will still enjoy the benefit of the sun which extends its universal bounty to all. He will still be in this way connected with the king in whose service he was prepared to lay down his life.

A very different reading of the same affirmation is however available to a more subtle analysis. Bolingbroke could be claiming equal, or even greater, status with Richard, under the same sun. If there is a distinction intended between 'warms' and 'shines' it could be a dangerous one. Where Richard is only comforted, rendered complacent, by the sun's flattering warmth, that sun of royal power may ultimately 'shine' on Bolingbroke, irradiating him with a greater luminosity. The word 'lent' is also a striking detail in its context. Is Richard's sun-like majesty merely a borrowed dignity? Does Bolingbroke envisage or anticipate a situation in which the sunlight of royal power begins to focus on him rather than on Richard? Is he already considering means by which the intended humiliation of his banishment may be turned into glory, and the sun of majesty persuaded to convert the bitter dust of exile into a golden crown of victory: 'Shall point on me, and gild my banishment'?

These questions are not set out to provoke straightforward answers. They are questions that lie unresolved within the ambiguous poetry of Bolingbroke's political discourse. We cannot provide simple, direct and definite answers to the questions aroused by an ambivalent language. Does Bolingbroke mean that he regards himself as a more likely candidate for the kingship than Richard? Or only that his family status and kinship ties make him more Richard's equal than his inferior? Does he ambiguously hint that his exile may be turned to his own benefit, making him popular and the king despised? Is that a definite bid for power, or a wish to see the balance of power between king and leading aristocracy restored? Does he imagine himself returning from exile in triumph, and Richard's power wilting before his own might? Or is he merely asserting that Richard's attempt to humiliate him will fail?

Obviously that critical view which seeks to explain Bolingbroke's motives by reference to supposed psychological absolutes such as 'ambition' has the tempting advantage of apparently simple explanations. In such terms there is no real ambiguity: there is falsehood on the surface, and underlying it there is truth. Bolingbroke has his eye on the crown, and the sub-text of his speech is a thinly veiled threat to the security of Richard's power. Only a habitual cautiousness and a pathological hypocrisy prevent Bolingbroke from making the threat directly.

If on the other hand we reject the presupposition that the truth is both simple and concealed, and pay more attention to the complex ambiguity of Bolingbroke's political language, then we may lose an apparent transparency of meaning but we gain a richness and complexity of dramatic experience. Suppose Bolingbroke really *doesn't* envisage the possible consequences of his actions? Suppose he is a man of clear and firm principles, who always acts in strict obedience to them, but lacks the intellectual sophistication and historical insight necessary to foresee what would happen if the traditional balance of power between king and aristocracy were to be pushed that little bit too far? After all, this struggle between Richard and the oppositional faction of powerful magnates has been going on for a long time, and has not up to now resulted in any radical or profound alteration in the basic structure of society. Why can it not continue indefinitely?

What I am suggesting is that Shakespeare depicted in Henry Bolingbroke a figure in many ways typical of his time, his class and his profession. A feudal aristocracy is a military caste, not a political élite; its profession is war, and its dominant ideology is the preservation of the system that maintains its power. It is precisely because Richard has attempted to change the system of feudal aristocracy that Bolingbroke needs to maintain political and military pressure upon him. All that Bolingbroke and his uncles Lancaster and York want is a restoration of the kind of social unity between aristocracy and monarch enjoyed under Edward III. They do not particularly want another king: they only want the king to operate in strict conformity with their own interests and their own authority. Should a member of the aristocracy find himself in occupation of a throne cleared of its incumbent by an excessive vigour of aristocratic opposition, he might well find himself in the invidious position of being obliged to think and act less like a rebellious baron, and more like an absolute monarch. The collapse of Richard's power actually brings such a situation into being; and it is Bolingbroke's fate to find himself reluctantly saddled with the responsibility of maintaining that royal power and prerogative claimed by Richard, and temporarily destroyed by Bolingbroke himself.

Bolingbroke's return from banishment is an action undertaken in overt defiance of the law, in flagrant disobedience of the royal power, and in open resistance to the king's authority. Is it the first move in a deliberately calculated campaign of rebellion, initiated with the ultimate intention of overthrowing Richard? That certainly seems to be the view of some of Bolingbroke's principal supporters, particularly Northumberland:

NORTHUMBERLAND
>If then we shall shake off our slavish yoke,
>Imp out our drooping country's broken wing,
>Redeem from broking pawn the blemished crown,
>Wipe off the dust that hides our sceptre's gilt,
>And make high majesty look like itself,
>Away with me in post to Ravenspurgh.

(II.1.291–6)

Northumberland clearly sees Bolingbroke as the potential leader of a movement capable of changing the face of England's monarchy. All the other lords involved in this conspiratorial conversation merely complain about Richard's misdeeds, and voice their own sense of injury. Northumberland, however, elaborates their straightforward language of social injustice and discontent into a more complex discourse. His poetic metaphors give emotional plangency, physical texture and substance to political notions such as national pride, resistance to injustice and the restoration of true majesty. This stirring vision of national resurgence is inseparable in Northumberland's political rhetoric from the aspiration to 'redeem' England's blemished crown – literally, to recover it from the power of those to whom Richard has pawned it – and to restore the nation's dignity by assisting Bolingbroke to overthrow Richard and to ascend the throne himself.

Northumberland's language is not Bolingbroke's, and it is a mistake to transpose the patent machiavellianism of the former to the political consciousness of the latter. When the returned Bolingbroke confronts his uncle, the Duke of York, it is with an insistence that his motives are limited to the ostensibly legitimate desire to have his inheritance restored. The point is made before York's appearance, when Lord Berkeley addresses him as 'my lord of Hereford'. Bolingbroke's reply is stiff with the punctilious pride of the aristocrat, sensitive to any word or gesture that seems to intend dishonour:

BOLINGBROKE
>My lord, my answer is to 'Lancaster'.
>And I am come to seek that name in England,
>And I must find that title in your tongue
>Before I make reply to aught you say.

(II.3.70–3)

The feeling that underlies that sensitivity, the wounded pride of the nobleman conscious of some serious personal or family injury, is perfectly appropriate to the expressed motive. York (who is, we remember,

63

acting as regent in Richard's absence) initially denounces his nephew in terms of a strict, straightforward and undeviating morality: Bolingbroke is a 'traitor' (II.3.87), his return from banishment 'gross rebellion and detested treason' (II.3.108). Bolingbroke's reply to this accusation is irresistibly persuasive because it invokes values and principles espoused by York himself (Bolingbroke's words echo closely York's remonstrance to Richard at II.1.189–208):

BOLINGBROKE

As I was banished, I was banished Hereford;
But as I come, I come for Lancaster.

. . .

If that my cousin King be King in England
It must be granted I am Duke of Lancaster.

(II.3.112–13, 122–3)

Bolingbroke supports the justice of his claim to recover his own rightful property and title, by appealing to the laws of inheritance. If Richard's inherited right to the crown holds good, then it cannot be denied that Bolingbroke has the right to inherit his father's title too. The legal reasons Bolingbroke puts forward constitute a persuasive and eloquently argued case: the king initially granted him 'letters patent' to seek his title in the courts, but now denies them; Bolingbroke ought to have the right to legal representation, but that is denied him too.

BOLINGBROKE

                              I am a subject,
And I challenge law. Attorneys are denied me,
And therefore personally I lay my claim
To my inheritance of free descent.

(II.3.132–5)

The appeals to law and justice are supported by more personal kinds of pleading, directed at York himself. Confronted by his rebellious nephew, York reminisces about the military exploits of his own youth, when he and Gaunt rescued the Black Prince from captivity by the French. He says that if he still possessed that kind of martial vigour, he would have no hesitation in dealing with Bolingbroke. But of course by naming Gaunt and alluding to the great heroic reputation of the family, York has named the very brother whose property Richard has expropriated and he has offered, in the stirring tale of epic achievement, yet another illustration of the injustice inflicted on the Lancastrian family. Bolingbroke invokes these details to substantiate an appeal to York's aristocratic values:

BOLINGBROKE
You are my father; for methinks in you
I see old Gaunt alive.

(II.3.116–17)

York cannot withstand these appeals to the very values he himself defended against Richard – 'I have had feeling of my cousin's wrongs' (II.3.140). His sense of loyalty to his family supersedes his loyalty to his sovereign. With some misgivings he wobbles into neutrality, but then immediately invites the rebel leaders to repose in the castle he himself is defending. From that point on, York remains with the rebels and resists them no further. He is won over not by constitutional arguments about the injustices of the king and the subject's right of resistance, but by simple visceral appeals to his profoundest loyalty, his love of kin and family.

Bolingbroke seems noticeably strengthened by York's capitulation. He can see the aristocratic clan coalescing once more into a unity of purpose and power. Act III opens with Bolingbroke in a commanding position, preparing to order the execution of the king's 'favourites', Bushy and Green, whom he condemns as 'caterpillars of the commonwealth' (II.3.165). Is he not here arrogating some of the supreme powers that properly belong to the king and the king's judicial authority? That is not in fact the impression we get of Bolingbroke's own perspective on the executions. His speech of condemnation defines very precisely the nature of his patriotism, the quality of his relationship with his 'England'. His political language is quite different from John of Gaunt's lyrical patriotism, and quite different from Richard's intimate and sentimental cherishing of his 'England' in the following scene. Bolingbroke's discourse is the solid, proprietary language of a nobleman talking about his estate. He charges the favourites with responsibility for misleading the king, for separating him from the queen (keeping him out of his bed, either by homosexual liaisons or simply by general debauchery) and for causing a breach in the friendship between the king and himself. Like the charges of embezzlement and conspiracy alleged against Mowbray, these allegations seem vague and uninteresting. They sound like gestures towards public justice, offered 'here in the view of men' primarily to exculpate Bolingbroke, to 'wash your blood / From off my hands' (III.1.5–6). Just as the specific charges against Mowbray collapse into the fundamental accusation of Gloucester's murder, so these generalized objections against Bushy and Green pale into insignificance beside the much more strongly worded account of the personal injuries sustained by Bolingbroke himself. This later part of the speech carries an accent of personal grudge and recrimination which is simultaneously an expression of wounded aristocratic pride. The damage has been done to Bolingbroke's property, but every detail is felt with an intense and hypersensitive consciousness of physical injury:

BOLINGBROKE
> Myself – a prince by fortune of my birth,
> Near to the King in blood, and near in love
> Till you did make him misinterpret me –
> Have stooped my neck under your injuries,
> And sighed my English breath in foreign clouds,
> Eating the bitter bread of banishment
> Whilst you have fed upon my signories,
> Disparked my parks, and felled my forest woods,
> From my own windows torn my household coat,
> Razed out my imprese, leaving me no sign
> Save men's opinions and my living blood
> To show the world I am a gentleman.

(III.1.16–27)

Bolingbroke thinks of his nationality, his 'Englishness', primarily in terms of his property, his estates. These personal possessions are the material attributes which help to constitute the identity of a 'gentleman'. 'Property' is sharply delineated by the clear, concrete images of parks, forests, emblazoned windows, coats-of-arms, personal heraldic symbols ('impreses'). The damage inflicted on them is felt as an injury sustained by the self. Although Bolingbroke appears to be acting here as if he is king already, and although within a very short time the whole of the realm will become his 'private property', the consciousness revealed by this political language is not that of a usurping regicide. It is that of a feudal aristocrat determined to recover his property, restore his status and re-establish the social conditions in which his family and his class can feel secure in their power and authority.

When Richard gives himself up at Flint Castle, Bolingbroke reiterates the simple legitimacy of his motives:

BOLINGBROKE
> My gracious lord, I come but for mine own.

(III.3.196)

Richard thinks differently:

KING RICHARD
> Up, cousin, up. Your heart is up, I know,
> Thus high at least, although your knee be low.

(III.3.194–5)

'Thus high at least': to the height of Richard's crown. Richard of course is the one who proves correct; but by this stage Richard's own peculiar collapse into self-abnegation, and his elaborate lyrical embracing of martyrdom, are almost promptings, cues for Bolingbroke's unfocused aspirations to key on to. If Bolingbroke did not have designs on the crown before, by the time he has listened to Richard's premature lamentations it would seem unlikely that he should remain entirely innocent of them.

Bolingbroke accepts the throne with a characteristically taciturn observation, frustrating our desire for open self-revelations:

BOLINGBROKE
> In God's name I'll ascend the regal throne.

(IV.1.113)

Is his accession such a foregone conclusion as to merit virtually no commentary at all? Or does Henry Bolingbroke become Henry IV with surprisingly little in the way of 'election addresses' or 'policy statements'? Is this the culmination of a long, protracted campaign of political aspiration? Or does he find himself almost unexpectedly catapulted to power, unprepared and tongue-tied by the sudden accession of enormous responsibility?

As the new king, Henry seems initially to manage the affairs of the kingdom efficiently and with reasonable success. He presides calmly over a boisterous parliament (IV.1), satisfies himself that Gloucester's murderer has met his end (IV.1.101–6), deals effectively with a dangerous conspiracy against him, patches up a quarrel within a noble family (V.3), and quells the last remnants of Ricardian resistance against his power (V.6.7–8). Yet the play closes with this irresistibly triumphant king planning a pilgrimage to the Holy Land, seeking in the language and imagery of a simple, world-shunning piety some absolution from the guilt of Richard's murder. Will the guilt of Richard's murder shadow and undermine Henry's kingship, as the guilt of Gloucester's murder shadowed Richard's?

3. Minor Characters

The term 'minor characters' can often be misleading when used as a means of analysing characterization in Shakespeare plays. Even where a play appears to be divided into hierarchically arranged levels of action, 'main-plot' and 'sub-plot', it does not necessarily follow that the occupants of the former will inevitably outweigh, in significance as well as in rank, the inhabitants of the latter. The next two plays in the historical cycle which is opened by *Richard II* – *Henry IV, Part 1* and *Henry IV, Part 2* – are disproportionately dominated by one character, Falstaff, who ought really to be innocuously confined to the comic 'sub-plot'.

The Elizabethan stage often came under attack from writers who represented a rather more educational intellectual tradition than the medium of popular entertainment for which Shakespeare and other dramatists wrote. One of the objections raised (for example, by Sir Philip Sidney) against the plays of the public theatres was that they tended to 'mingle kings and clowns', to jumble indiscriminately together things which ought by the rules of neo-classical literary and dramatic theory to be kept rigidly segregated. But it was the very nature of Elizabethan popular drama – and of the public stages on which these plays were enacted, where scenes alternated very rapidly, and characters entering brushed shoulders with others making their exit – for all the elements in a dramatic world to be mingled promiscuously together.

Now *Richard II* is actually rather unlike any other history play by Shakespeare in that it seems closer to that educated milieu where people thought of drama as an art which ought to be confined to a system of rules. In form and structure the play more closely resembles Christopher Marlowe's *Edward II*, which was probably written earlier than Shakespeare's play. (Marlowe, without any real justification, except that he went to university, was popularly thought of as more learned than Shakespeare.)

There are no comic characters, no 'clowns' to mingle with the kings; there is only one main action, unaccompanied by any complementary 'sub-plot', and punctuated only by the formal and ritualistic garden-scene. Another way of describing it would be to say that *Richard II* is more strictly and comprehensively a historical play than any other of Shakespeare's histories. Whatever freedom of imaginative invention the dramatist left space for, all the events of the play (with the single exception of the garden-scene) are derived from historically verifiable circumstances. As a result, we do not even have the convenience of a division of plots to help us determine the difference between major and minor characters; and if the dramatic world of the play is really so homogeneous and uniformly imagined, it is possible that all the characters (apart from the gardeners, and the odd character who pops up momentarily according to the 'now-you-see-me-now-you-don't' system of dramatic participation, like the Welsh Captain in II.4) have some important role to enact in the composition of the play's historical world.

Now of course there is one character in the play who clearly dominates the entire action, and in some ways towers over everyone else in significance: that is, Richard himself. As we have seen, Richard makes himself into a major character, not only by asserting his supremacy when in power, but paradoxically by dominating in defeat. It is certainly possible to see the play as structured by Richard's rise and downfall; to read it, in other words, as a tragedy, in which we would expect a particular character, the tragic hero (Macbeth, Hamlet, Othello, Lear) to appear isolated within the painful intensity of his tragic crisis and defeat. When *Richard II* was first printed, it was defined by the title-page as a 'tragedy'.

We will examine the implications of such a definition in the last chapter. Where, in the meantime, would Bolingbroke stand if we thought of Richard as individuated and isolated by the play's tragic form? Would he be too big for a minor, not quite big enough for a major character? In fact of course, as our previous discussion will indicate, Richard's rise and downfall are inextricably linked, perfectly complemented and finely balanced by Bolingbroke's fall and subsequent rise: the two 'mighty opposites' are perpetually locked together in a dialectical conflict. This of course represents another way of looking at the play, which we might call a 'political' reading. In this case the main action, the principal dramatic structure, is not the ascendence and collapse of the tragic hero, but the interpenetrating, linking and diverging fortunes of the two great political rivals.

Although *Richard II* was categorized as a 'tragedy' on its title-page, when Shakespeare's plays were published together in the first 'collected works', the 'First Folio' of 1623, it was included among the 'history' plays. This brings us to a third possible way of reading the play's overall form and structure. If the central action of the play is not the narrative of any individual psychological history, but a historical action in which individuals perform actions of general significance and historical import, then the 'status' of an individual may be easier to define by the general historical action in which all are engaged, than by reference to some system of measuring individuals for their value as 'characters'. John of Gaunt is dead by the end of II.1, but his historical importance immensely outweighs his physical presence in the play. The Bishop of Carlisle only has one scene in which he figures with any kind of impact, but his great speech of historical prophecy, predicting a civil war as the inevitable consequence of deposing Richard, has profound historical reverberations and is echoed throughout the whole series of plays up to *Henry V*.

We do not have to choose which one of these readings – the play as tragedy, political drama or history play – is correct or most appropriate. Clearly *Richard II* has elements of all three, and can be read in the light of these and of other theoretical approaches. The Elizabethan dramatists who like Shakespeare wrote mainly for the public theatres certainly did not think of these genres as clearly demarcated or strictly segregated. They would often, for example, call a play a 'historical tragedy' or 'tragical history'. We should think of these generic definitions simply as perspectives, angles from which we can look at a play and see its structure and composition falling into different patterns of dramatic meaning. In looking at the 'minor' characters then, I am assuming that a character may have a substantial role to play in the historical action without necessarily commanding a great deal of stage time, or having a lot of lines to speak. This chapter will deal with the older generation of aristocrats, Lancaster, York and Northumberland; with the female characters, Queen Isabel, the Duchess of Gloucester and the Duchess of York; and with the gardeners of III.4.

Lancaster, York, Northumberland

As we have already seen, John of Gaunt, Duke of Lancaster, is a loyal though reluctant supporter of the crown and of his nephew's royal authority. His brother Edmund Langley, Duke of York, occupies a similiar position of qualified loyalty, but is dislodged from it by the force of events and ends up supporting the baronial rebellion. The Earl of Northumberland represents a different political position. He is from the outset a determined opponent of Richard's kingship, and proves a ruthless and unscrupulous campaigner to have Richard overthrown.

These three great magnates seem to fall into a clear pattern of difference: each represents a contrasting approach to the problems of divided loyalty thrown up by Richard's style of government. Yet we will find, if we examine them as a group, that they share attitudes and values as much as they differ in temperament and personal style. They share, above all, a common animosity towards Richard's rule; and that aristocratic and anti-monarchical hostility constitutes the ideology of the baronial class as Shakespeare conceived its historical character.

It is natural to think of John of Gaunt as a great supporter of absolute monarchical power. Outside the play his famous patriotic speech in celebration of 'this royal throne of kings ... this England' has certainly been employed to support the authority of many subsequent British kings and governments. It is important to remember that in the play this speech actually functions as a diatribe of criticism against the ruling monarch, and that Gaunt is not, as we usually assume, depicting the England of the present, but expressing a nostalgic regret for an England long since vanished into the historical past. It is precisely because the England he sees before him – Richard's England – falls so far short of his idealized vision of what he believes England once was, that his poetic vision of national glory is so brightly and vividly imagined:

JOHN OF GAUNT

This royal throne of kings, this sceptred isle,
This earth of majesty, this seat of Mars,
This other Eden – demi-paradise –
This fortress built by nature for herself
Against infection and the hand of war,
This happy breed of men, this little world,
This precious stone set in the silver sea,
Which serves it in the office of a wall,
Or as a moat defensive to a house
Against the envy of less happier lands;
This blessèd plot, this earth, this realm, this England,
This nurse, this teeming womb of royal kings,
Feared by their breed, and famous by their birth,
Renownèd for their deeds as far from home
For Christian service and true chivalry
As is the sepulchre in stubborn Jewry
Of the world's ransom, blessèd Mary's son ...

(II.1.40–56)

The realm of England is here defined largely in terms of its monarchy, its history distinguished by the quality of its kings: 'royal throne of kings', 'earth of majesty', 'teeming womb of royal kings'. But the monarchs Gaunt idealizes are not like Richard. They are kings like Richard Coeur-de-lion, or Gaunt's father Edward III – great warrior kings 'renownèd for their deeds', famous exponents of 'Christian service and true chivalry'.

These are the warlike, crusading, feudal kings of the early Middle Ages, so Gaunt's speech is after all no panegyric of royal absolutism, but a lament for the passing of a feudal kingdom in which king and nobility were united by a natural balance of forces into a 'happy breed of men'.

The image of the crusade is a symbol for this perfect synthesis of king and nobility. It crops up, in one form or another, throughout the subsequent plays in this historical series. And we see that at the end of *Richard II*, and at the beginning of the next play *Henry IV, Part 1*, Henry IV (Bolingbroke that was) nostagically imagines that the only means of healing the bitter divisions of the society is to re-enact, in the form of a pilgrimage or crusade to Jerusalem, the social unity of the old feudal kingdom.

Gaunt's speech is not merely an appeal for strong leadership in the king, and it is certainly not a defence of the Renaissance doctrine of divine right and absolute royal authority. On the contrary, he imagines royal authority as inseparable from the power of the nobility; the golden age he longs for and regrets is that of a feudalism held together by the authority of a strong king *and* by the power of a strong aristocracy. Gaunt's attack on Richard's style of government concentrates on the fact that Richard has replaced the feudal bonds of 'fealty' – the system of reciprocal obligations which bind lord and subject in a feudal polity – with economic contracts:

JOHN OF GAUNT
  England, bound in with the triumphant sea,

              . . .

              is now bound in with shame,
  With inky blots and rotten parchment bonds.

                                 (II.1.61, 63–4)

Richard is now a mere 'landlord' of England, rather than a king. He has sought to dispense with the loyal co-operation of the nobility, and to rule with the assistance of an upstart bureaucracy of 'favourites'. Determined to shake off the influence of the barons, he has introduced radical economic policies to raise revenue without reliance on the great landholders. On Gaunt's death Richard illustrates both his commitment to such policies and his refusal to accept Gaunt's counsel by confiscating his estates. Thus we can see that the unacceptability of Richard's kingship consists, in Gaunt's eyes, in his modernizing programme of de- feudalization, and his consequent slighting of the traditional aristocracy.

It is ironic that so many subsequent appeals to English patriotism have been mounted on the basis of this statement of baronial self-interest: this celebration of a class that has scarcely earned the unqualified admiration of even the most conservative of thinkers.

The Duke of York is conventionally thought of as a very different character from his brother. Where Lancaster stands up against the king, York remains silent. Where Gaunt refuses to compromise on the point of loyalty to the legitimate sovereign, York eventually joins the rebellion. These indications seem to point to a contrast between weakness and strength, and to an interpretation of York's character as that of a fussy and indecisive senior civil servant. In actual fact Lancaster and York experience exactly the same self-division with regard to Richard's kingship. They have both maintained their loyalty in the face of severe provocation; they both criticize Richard for the murder of Gloucester, for his reliance on his favourites and his rejection of the nobility, for his unorthodox attitudes towards property and inheritance. Gaunt's self-division is resolved by his death: York has to carry his divided loyalties into new historical conditions.

In response to Richard's confiscation of Bolingbroke's inheritance, York voices exactly the same feelings and values as those which underpin Gaunt's ideology. He also regrets the passing of the old warrior class of militaristic kings (II.1.171–9); and his anger at the expropriation of his brother's property prompts him to a bold and principled restatement of the baronial perspective:

YORK
    Take Hereford's rights away, and take from Time
    His charters and his customary rights.
    Let not tomorrow then ensue today.
    Be not thyself; for how art thou a king
    But by fair sequence and succession?

                                         (II.1.195–9)

The 'order' of the kingdom is, for York, guaranteed not by strong and assertive royal government, but by a mutual and agreed respect for law and tradition. Again the kind of social contract that is being affirmed, and that the king has disrupted, is the feudal relationship in which the king was bound by reciprocal bonds of fealty to respect and protect the rights of the subject. Richard has demanded from his subjects simple obedience, the requirement of the absolute monarch. Both Gaunt and York have argued, quite in the spirit of Magna Charta, that the king must observe constitutional restraints on his own power and prerogative;

and that if his subjects are not granted the rights which they themselves can legally and morally expect, they may find themselves, however unwillingly, pushed into rebellion.

YORK

If you do wrongfully seize Hereford's rights

. . .

You lose a thousand well-disposèd hearts,
And prick my tender patience to those thoughts
Which honour and allegiance cannot think.

(II.1.201, 206–8)

Bolingbroke's return from banishment prompts York to a clear expression of baronial self-division.

YORK

Both are my kinsmen.
T'one is my sovereign, whom both my oath
And duty bids defend. T'other again
Is my kinsman, whom the King hath wronged,
Whom conscience and my kindred bids to right.

(II.2.111–15)

Two equally valid but incompatible allegiances add up not to an indecisive character, but to a historical contradiction.

The Earl of Northumberland represents a much simpler case, since for him there is no problem of loyalty: his allegiance is to the traditional aristocracy, and for him the king's manifest injustices legitimate the subject's resistance. Northumberland holds exactly the same point of view as Gaunt and York with respect to Richard's kingship. He regrets the demise of the old warrior kings (II.1.252–5), the decline of the nobility and the influence of upstart favourites (II.1.238–45), and he objects to Richard's expropriation of the Lancastrian inheritance as an unforgivable offence and insult to the aristocracy (II.1.224–7). Northumberland experiences no problem of divided allegiance, since he believes that a king who acts as Richard has done can no longer legitimately exact obedience from the subject. Since the subjects in question are not Elizabethan or modern private citizens, but medieval warlords able to muster and command private armies, the capacity for rebellion, joined with the political will, is well within the aristocracy's power. Northumberland is usually thought of as Shakespeare's classic portrayal of the 'machiavel', the unscrupulous and opportunistic politician, and if one considers details such as Northumberland's abject flat-

tery of Bolingbroke (II.3.1–18), his hypocritical protestations of innocence (III.3.101–20), and his ruthless insistence on Richard's signing
the faked confession (IV.1.222ff.), he seems to well deserve that title.
But if we permit Northumberland's serious espousal of specific historical
ideas, shared also by Lancaster and York, to be dissolved into some
generalized notion of the eternal politician, we immediately lose the rich
historical texture of the drama, and we find ourselves in possession of a
play whose apparent modernity of appeal barely conceals its artistic and
ideological thinness.

The women

In one of the key scenes of the play, King Richard marks his departure
from the stage by speaking, almost as an afterthought, to his Queen
Isabel:

KING RICHARD
  Come on, our Queen; tomorrow must we part.
  Be merry; for our time of stay is short.

(II.1.222–3)

A reader of the printed play-text (as distinct from the spectator of a
performance) could be forgiven for wondering, at least momentarily,
where this queen came from. Only saying a brief sentence herself she
has not been spoken or even referred to in the course of the 150 or so
lines during which she occupies the stage. It is actually necessary to
look back to the stage-direction which announces the arrival of the
king (at line 68) to see that the queen enters with the king and a group
of nobles. For the reader of the play (whose attention is necessarily
focused on those characters who manifest their presence in speech), a
self-effacing character, who is also ignored by everyone else in the
room, simply does not exist. In a stage production of course things
are different. The text calls for the queen to be physically, visibly
present among the king's entourage, and her passive presence could
actually be made quite significant. But when deciding what to do with
the queen, actors and directors are left entirely to their own devices,
reliant on the resources of their own imaginations; the verbal text
itself has nothing whatsoever to say about the strange, virtually silent
presence of Queen Isabel.

Act II.1 involves eleven characters, only one of whom – the queen – is
female. That disproportionate marginalization of the female population
is typical of this play as a whole. Only five female characters, which

includes the ladies attending Queen Isabel in the garden-scene, appear in a cast of over thirty identified parts (not counting various supernumerary servants, attendants and soldiers, who are also overwhelmingly male). These are the Duchess of Gloucester, who appears only in I.2 (her death is then reported in II.2, line 97); the Duchess of York, who appears only in V.2 and 3; and the queen, who appears in three scenes – II.2, III.4, V.1 – in addition to her presence in II.1.

Now a number of common-sense arguments naturally present themselves to suggest that there is really nothing remarkable in this. There is never more than a handful of female parts in any of Shakespeare's plays, a fact obviously connected with the Elizabethan practice of using boys to play the roles of women. *Richard II* is a history play, and Elizabethan history plays were drawn from historical writings which did not particularly emphasize the presence or agency of women in history: history was largely thought of as an account of the actions of men. Lastly, this particular historical drama deals with the kind of political and military crises which necessarily excluded women from active participation: political struggles, trials by combat, military campaigns. That exclusion of women from the decisive and determinant activities of a society is something we would naturally, from the perspective of modern ideas, decry. But it is a historical injustice for which we can hardly blame Shakespeare. In the historical story of the deposition of Richard II, the playwright found no remarkable or influential women, so that absence was duly and dutifully reflected in the play.

A moment's consideration will reveal that all these apparently 'common-sense' arguments are extremely suspect. It is a fact that only a small number of female roles is to be found in Elizabethan plays. But the women characters who occupy those roles usually have a disproportionate influence within the world of the play: Viola, Rosalind, Portia, Cordelia, Desdemona, Lady Macbeth. It is often even the case that they show strengths and abilities, kinds of determination and resourcefulness, not displayed by their menfolk. As we witness Portia dominating and winning Antonio's trial in *The Merchant of Venice*, or Cordelia leading an army in *King Lear*, or Lady Macbeth returning to the murdered Duncan's chamber in *Macbeth*, we are unlikely to derive from Shakespeare's plays any simple notion of women as 'the weaker sex'. This is certainly not the case in *Richard II*, where the queen is a pathetic melancholy spectator of her husband's downfall.

As we have seen, the Elizabethan dramatist's relationship with his historical sources was not a passive and automatic subservience. Although the Tudor period saw the emergence of a modern conception of historical 'fact' (Samuel Daniel, author of a long poem about the Wars of the Roses which Shakespeare seems to have used, carefully distinguished between authentic historical fact and imaginative fiction), all the history plays of this period mingle fact with interpretation, historical authenticity with imaginative elaboration. When Shakespeare dramatized other periods of history in which women are described as significant figures, he gave them even more prominent roles – Joan of Arc and Queen Margaret in the *Henry VI* plays are obvious examples. After *Richard II* Shakespeare started to interpolate fictional comic sub-plots into the 'factual' material of the chronicle drama, thus providing more space for the participation of women. In the *Henry IV* plays, women like the Hostess and Doll Tearsheet have active and important (if distinctly 'low-life') roles to play. So Shakespeare was quite free to make more of Queen Isabel than the historical sources themselves warranted. In fact he did, since the young woman who appears in the play to express her unfocused melancholy, to complain of her husband's declining fortunes, and to lament his tragic overthrow, has no real historical authority at all. Isabel was a child of ten when these events occurred. Her passive role in the play is then, we might say, historically appropriate; her dramatic characterization is all Shakespeare's invention.

The third argument from 'common sense', that the particular historical character of this action excludes the active agency of women in a particularly decisive and intractable way, has rather more force. It is one thing to invent an interesting dramatic character for Isabel: but if women in the fourteenth century did not (outside chivalric romances) take part in chivalric combats, Shakespeare could hardly clap his queen in armour and let her fight the king's battles for him. Those active and enterprising heroines who appear in other Shakespeare plays seem to belong to an age when a formidable 'queen' showed herself capable (in a sense) of fighting her own battles, such as that against the Spanish Armada. They appear naturally sympathetic to our own later age in which the principle of female equality, though hardly universally attained, is at least generally accepted. Mowbray's words, and Isabel's character, belong rather to that post-feudal society of the late fourteenth century in which, according to the dominant systems of belief, men were warriors and women were a protected species.

It seems to me possible that the marginalization of women in a play like *Richard II* is not simply the symptomatic expression of an unconscious misogyny, or a passive reflection of pre-determined historical conditions. It is rather a historical reality that the play foregrounds, interrogates and criticizes. Women may not be much in evidence in the play, but femininity is. Let us take a closer look at the scene with which we began (II.1), the scene of Isabel's strangely absent presence. As I noted above, Isabel appears there in a scene populated otherwise entirely by men. The problems and issues debated in the scene are specifically 'masculine' preserves: politics, war, economics, law, property. Throughout the scene what the characters say about their specific situation carries with it wider dimensions of reference, so that other groups of people are continually being alluded to and moving into temporary focus. Again, these are all groups of men. Young men, sick men, dying men, living men, flattering courtiers, lawyers, Englishmen ('this happy breed'), Frenchmen, Irishmen, fathers, grandfathers, brothers, sons, uncles, kings, knights, commons, nobles, ancestors, 'men of war'. It would be hard to imagine a world more thoroughly cleared of any sign of the female gender.

Yet if we look a little closer, vestigial traces of femininity begin to surface: the repressed returns. John of Gaunt sings the praises of that 'happy breed of men'(II.1.45) who under the strong government of warrior kings like Edward III had excelled in the conquest of other nations. Englishmen are famous for their strength, their military successes, their masculinity. But to describe a category of men, however unimpeachably manly, as a 'breed', is to draw attention to the fact that somehow they must have been 'bred', and therefore that members of the female sex must have played something more than a marginal role in the process. Gaunt also talks about 'birth' (II.1.52), though there he is perhaps talking less about the biological process by which children are delivered than about the male-dominated dynastic system of lineage. More distinctively revealing are his references to England as a 'nurse' and as a 'teeming womb of royal kings' (II.1.51), metaphors which draw attention to the specifically female capacities of gestation and suckling. As Gaunt's celebration of the achievements of the English aristocracy extends to include the Crusades, he actually finds space to mention a woman's name:

GAUNT
   ... this teeming womb of royal kings,
   Feared by their breed, and famous by their birth,
   Renownèd for their deeds as far from home
   For Christian service and true chivalry
   As is the sepulchre in stubborn Jewry
   Of the world's ransom, blessèd Mary's son ...

                                  (II.1.51–6)

The allusion to the Virgin Mary is perhaps representative of Gaunt's view of women. Whatever cults of worship may attach to Mary, her primary significance is the fact that she gave birth to a remarkable man, Jesus. In Gaunt's feudal and aristocratic perspective, women appear as the passive vehicles by means of which the patriarchal seed is procreated, the patrilineal dynasty secured. Even the femininity of his metaphorical 'England' is ultimately spurious, since that maternal symbol is so completely a construction of the kings and warriors who have served their country in loyalty, fidelity and truth. None the less, however strenuous Gaunt's efforts to suppress the reality of the feminine, it continues to appear, if only in the interstices of his metaphorical language. You cannot really talk about nurses and wombs and birth and breeding without bringing into play a feminine dimension of meaning. Once that meaning occupies a space inside the imaginative universe of the play, it proves remarkably hard to expel.

We will now examine the part played in the drama by its three principal female characters. All three are present in the play not in their own right, or because they have any distinctive individual contribution to make to the play's action, but in terms of their relationships with men. They are all, primarily and even exclusively, wives and mothers. The Duchess of Gloucester is there to lament and preserve the memory of her murdered husband. The Duchess of York is there to plead, successfully, for the life of Aumerle her son. Queen Isabel has literally nothing to do in the play except to feel sadness and pity for her husband.

The Duchess of Gloucester, though restricted like Isabel to a melancholy choric role, is none the less a formidable portrait of female assertiveness, which is however ultimately deflected and turned to self-destructive grief and melancholy. The qualities she displays are those which in the gender-divided world of this play seem the peculiar prerogative of men. She is a fierce defender of the aristocratic royal family also celebrated by Gaunt and York; she asserts the responsibilities of aristocratic pride and status; she hungers for direct and immediate blood-revenge to appease the injuries to her family; and she advocates a military resistance to Richard's tyranny.

DUCHESS OF GLOUCESTER
   That which in mean men we entitle patience
   Is pale cold cowardice in noble breasts.
   What shall I say? To safeguard thine own life
   The best way is to venge my Gloucester's death.

                                (I.2.33–6)

But the Duchess's very strength and courage are self-denying, self-annihilating, since the noble family she idealizes, the dynasty of Edward III, consists entirely of men. The role of women in the composition of this dynasty is silently effaced, and they have no place or position in the family tree. The royal 'blood' that privileges and sacralizes the aristocratic family is a peculiarly masculine substance: it can either be spilt by murder, or redeemed by blood-revenge. Christian patience is scornfully dismissed as the natural subjection of the common, the 'mean' man; for the aristocratic subject, *noblesse oblige* – nobility carries obligations – and principal among those duties is the responsibility for avenging the death of a murdered kinsman.

The Duchess seeks to persuade Gaunt to take revenge against Richard but Gaunt is committed to preserving the security of the crown, however much he may disapprove of the particular king who wears it. The Duchess's hopes of revenge focus therefore on the possibility of Bolingbroke's emerging victorious from the combat with Mowbray. If Bolingbroke were to kill Mowbray, then a kinsman of Gloucester's would have succeeded in killing his murderer, and in casting a guilty shadow over the instigator of the murder, Richard himself. Revenge would be satisfied, her dead husband's ghost appeased.

DUCHESS OF GLOUCESTER
> O, sit my husband's wrongs on Hereford's spear
> That it may enter butcher Mowbray's breast!
> Or if misfortune miss the first career,
> Be Mowbray's sins so heavy in his bosom
> That they may break his foaming courser's back
> And throw the rider headlong in the lists,
> A caitiff recreant to my cousin Hereford!

(I.2.47–53)

Such militant violence of language proves the Duchess capable of that hot-blooded martial vigour defined by Mowbray in the opening scene as the peculiar prerogative of the male sex. For her, the wager of battle to be fought between Mowbray and Bolingbroke is not a legal process to determine guilt and innocence, not a litmus test for the detection of treachery. It is an opportunity for the prosecution of private revenge.

Despite her masculine imagery of chivalry, revenge and violence, the Duchess is prevented by her sex from acting in person to promote any of these desired ends. She can only ask men to act for her. Her femininity is negated twice over, first in her espousal of masculine feelings and values that repress the female, and second in the social prohibitions restraining her from taking any personal role in the activities she deems essential if her personal honour – which is defined entirely in terms of the honour of the men to whom she is related – is to be effectively defended. Her energies of principle and pride thus frustrated, they turn inwards with a damaging impact upon her vital self-esteem – 'Grief boundeth where it falls' (I.2.58) – and produce the emptiness and inconsolable sorrow that destroy her – 'Desolate, desolate will I hence and die' (I.2.74).

Sadness and melancholy are the natural fate of women in this play. Our introduction to Queen Isabel is to a mood of unfocused sadness, a grief without cause, which yet proves to be a prophetic monitor of imminent calamity. Isabel naturally uses the imagery of pregnancy and birth, but displaces such possibilities from her own body, envisaging the birth of nothing but misfortune:

QUEEN ISABEL
Some unborn sorrow ripe in fortune's womb
Is coming towards me . . .

(II.2.10–11)

Silent in her husband's presence, when left alone on Richard's departure to Ireland the queen is released to self-expression. But her only experience is that of self-abnegation, since she is possessed by a vague melancholy which seems both a disproportionate response to her lord's absence, and an ominous foreboding of his impending tragedy. When Green brings the news of Bolingbroke's return from banishment, that phantom pregnancy is delivered of its burden of sorrow.

QUEEN ISABEL
So, Green, thou art the midwife to my woe,
And Bolingbroke my sorrow's dismal heir.
Now hath my soul brought forth her prodigy,
And I, a gasping new-delivered mother,
Have woe to woe, sorrow to sorrow joined.

(II.2.62–6)

Isabel's 'inward soul' (II.2.11 and 28) seems to contain nothing of her own, only grief for the absence or future suffering of another. To describe this experience of unfocused sorrow awaiting a cause to which it may be attached, the queen uses the imagery of pregnancy and birth. Isabel means that her prophetic sadness joins with her real sorrow to give her a double 'woe'; but also that as a 'mother' whose symbolic confinement delivers her of a tragic destiny, she also suffers twice – from the pain of childbirth, and from the pain of discovering her 'child' to be the 'prodigy' of Bolingbroke's usurpation. Isabel's language specifically draws attention to the way in which women in this play are condemned to suffering by the patriarchism of the aristocratic dynasty. Their only function in this masculine world is that of bearing sons for their powerful husbands; so that even in the successful achievement of their biological function, their own lives are negated. The more illustrious and legendary the lives of their husbands and sons, the more completely are they themselves eclipsed from the significant structure of the family. Isabel's lot is particularly hard, since she will not bear Richard's children (the historical Isabel was a child of ten when these events occurred): her 'dismal heir' (II.2.63) is the succession of Bolingbroke. Deprived by fate of what is seen as the only kind of power women can possess – the capacity to reproduce powerful men – Isabel's life seems unspeakably and inconsolably sad. In place of the child she will not bear, the Gardener plants in elegiac remembrance of her sorrow a 'bank of rue':

GARDENER
Rue even for ruth here shortly shall be seen
In the remembrance of a weeping Queen.

(III.4.106–7)

In the queen's last scene (V.1), where she takes leave of the deposed king, Isabel laments Richard's fall, and in doing so she acknowledges the blossom of her own life to be 'withered':

QUEEN ISABEL
But soft, but see, or rather do not see,
My fair rose wither.

(V.1.7 8)

Again, her function is quite literally marginal: to stand by the roadside to observe the 'woeful pageant' of the king's disgrace. Here however Isabel makes her one display of strength, manifesting that potentiality for resistance already seen in the Duchess of Gloucester:

QUEEN ISABEL
The lion dying thrusteth forth his paw
And wounds the earth, if nothing else, with rage
To be o'erpowered. And wilt thou pupil-like
Take the correction, mildly kiss the rod . . .?

(V.1.29 32)

But whatever reserves of strength and defiance the woman has, she cannot act for herself. She can only ask men to act for her. Richard's response to this encouragement is to declare that he is, in effect, already dead, and the queen already ('Good sometimes queen', V.1.37) a widow.

The other main female character in the play, the Duchess of York, offers what is in effect a contrasting success story, precisely because she accepts and embraces the subjected and marginal role of women. Her significance is that she is mother to Aumerle, the close companion and supporter of Richard who joins the Abbot of Westminster's conspiracy against the life of Henry. She is a mother, now past the age of child-bearing. The prospect of losing her son would rob her of her very exist-ence, reduce her to the shadowy unreality of the childless Isabel:

DUCHESS OF YORK
    Is not my teeming-date drunk up with time?
    And wilt thou pluck my fair son from mine age?
    And rob me of a happy mother's name?

(V.2.91–3)

In her appeal to her husband to save their son, the Duchess brings out the contradictions of this patriarchal maternity. Her suffering in child-birth to deliver Aumerle predisposes her to a pity her husband cannot feel:

DUCHESS OF YORK
    Hadst thou groaned for him as I have done
    Thou wouldst be more pitiful.

(V.2.103–4)

Although she does not question the patriarchal principle that a woman's only proper profession is that of bearing sons, the Duchess does at least suggest that femininity may have its own peculiar experiences and values, in some ways quite separate from the world of masculine ideology. But this potential affirmation of femininity is soon eclipsed, since in order to save Aumerle the Duchess has to plead with men, and to argue on their terms. She tries to persuade York that Aumerle resembles only him, not her or any of her relatives:

DUCHESS OF YORK
    He is as like thee as a man may be;
    Not like to me, or any of my kin . . .

(V.2.109–10)

To save her son the Duchess is not only prepared to humiliate herself – 'For ever will I walk upon my knees' (V.3.92) – but even to sacrifice the personal traces of her maternal inheritance: only as the exclusive property of his father will Aumerle appear to be worth saving. Though she resists her husband, who is determined to incriminate his son, the Duchess can do so only by appealing to a greater, symbolic father, who represents the paternalistic principle of divinity ('God the father') in mortal form, the king: 'A god on earth thou art!' (V.3.135).

The play's representation of its female characters shows quite clearly that in this male-dominated society women are consistently marginalized and subjected to a passive social role. They are the instruments and vehicles of masculine power, possessing no effective or positive social identity of their own. This severe limitation on the active presence of women, which is so unusual in Shakespeare's plays, seems to me an aspect of the play's historical vision. This is the unenviable lot of women in a feudal, patriarchal and chivalric society. They may be romanticized as mothers or idealized as lovers, but in themselves they are nothing – they derive their significance only from their relationships with husbands, brothers, sons. It is not a representation of the natural lot of women, or a depiction of women as they existed in Shakespeare's England, where the most powerful member of society was after all, a woman, Queen Elizabeth.

The condition of female self-abnegation provokes a consistent and comprehensive response of pity and compassion, like the Gardener's planting, in elegiac remembrance of Isabel's sorrow, of a bank of the herb rue, symbol of sadness and regret. And when Bushy in II.2 attempts to comfort and console the queen's nameless grief, he unwittingly discloses the strange and insubstantial existence allowed to women by this feudal and patriarchal society. In an elaborate conceit, Bushy argues that grief and sorrow multiply themselves into numerous 'shadows', so that when observed from an angle, like perspective paintings, they appear greater than their real substance. The queen's sadness at her lord's departure is thus exaggerated into a disproportionate anxiety. But how then is the sufferer supposed to distinguish shadow from substance, reality from illusion? If Isabel looks correctly at the real conditions of her life, she will see '. . . naught but shadows / Of what it is not' (II.2.23–4). Thus we see the woman's life de-realized by the very pity that is offered as her consolation.

The play reveals quite clearly that in this kind of patriarchal society, dominated by powerful men and their concerns, women have a purely marginal function. It cannot convincingly be argued that the play simply presents that condition as natural and unremarkable, since the women in the play are the objects of a powerful sense of pity. Of course it is easier to offer pity than to secure justice. It could be argued that Shakespeare's own ideology is as patriarchal as John of Gaunt's, since the play cannot imagine women as anything other than the instruments of men and the bearers and protectors of male children: the saddest thing that can be said of a woman is that she has no children. Feminist critics would argue that this kind of pity is a more dangerous enemy to the cause of female emancipation than open injustice. Though it appears to have the interests of women at heart, it still cannot conceive of women as anything other than the passive instruments of masculine oppression or compassion.

This is really the point where the debate begins. My own conviction is that the play can be read as demonstrative of a deep-seated structural injustice in the way this society positions women. If we read the play historically, we can see that it goes further than the utterance of mere compassion for the unfulfilled lives of its female characters. It reveals quite clearly that as long as women are positioned in society in the way they are here, there can be no realization or fulfilment of female existence. Whether a woman has children or is denied them, whether her husband is successful or a failure, the woman's own life remains empty and sterile. In V.3 Bolingbroke, now Henry IV, reveals for the first time that he has a son: the young Prince Henry, who will not appear in this play, but whose personal and political development will be the principal subject of the remaining plays in this historical sequence. There is nowhere in this play, or in any of the others, a specific reference to Prince Henry having a mother, Bolingbroke a wife. The child is his father's son.

The gardeners

The garden-scene, III.4., is a unique moment in *Richard II*. It is a distinct pause in the action, the only interruption in an otherwise unbroken historical narrative. It is the only part of the play that features characters and an action not to be found in the history books. Lastly, it is a scene of extreme formality and overt, obtrusive symbolism, elaborately conventional and emblematic, which falls quite outside any possibility of realistic reading or naturalistic performance. The scene begins with the queen and her attendants (in the Folio text 'two ladies') trying to think of something to do. They are joined on stage by the Gardener and his two servants, who appear to have plenty to do. We begin then with a parallelism and a contrast. The two groups of characters mirror each other, men and women, a similar grouping in each case. The women are idle and unoccupied courtiers; the men craftsmen or workers.

Many interpretations of the scene have taken their cue from the foregrounded parallelism, and from the queen's introductory remark:

QUEEN ISABEL
  But stay, here come the gardeners.

. . .

  They will talk of state; for everyone doth so
  Against a change.

(III.4.24, 27–8)

This seems to suggest an explanation for the Gardener's interest in politics ('state') where we might expect him to be more interested in gardening. In fact when the Gardener does begin to speak, it is gardening that he talks about:

GARDENER
  Go, bind thou up young dangling apricocks
  Which, like unruly children, make their sire
  Stoop with oppression of their prodigal weight.
  Give some supportance to the bending twigs.
  Go thou, and like an executioner
  Cut off the heads of too fast-growing sprays
  That look too lofty in our commonwealth.
  All must be even in our government.

(III.4.29–36)

Since one does not normally talk about the 'government' of a garden, the queen's prediction is obviously correct. The Gardener appears as a symbol of the political leader, his garden the commonwealth, his craft of gardening a metaphorical form of 'government'. The servant who replies to the Gardener's commands starts to disentangle the threads of metaphor into more self-explanatory simile:

FIRST MAN
  Why should we, in the compass of a pale,
  Keep law and form and due proportion,
  Showing as in a model our firm estate,
  When our sea-wallèd garden, the whole land,
  Is full of weeds, her fairest flowers choked up,
  Her fruit trees all unpruned, her hedges ruined,
  Her knots disordered, and her wholesome herbs
  Swarming with caterpillars?

(III.4.40–47)

'. . . our sea-wallèd garden, the whole land' clearly poses the terms of the comparison, as well as echoing John of Gaunt's earlier 'this England' speech. The literal 'caterpillars' that prove a nuisance in the garden recall those 'caterpillars of the commonwealth' which Bolingbroke swore to 'weed and pluck away' (II.3.166). The Gardener then refers explicitly to Bolingbroke's execution of Richard's favourites:

GARDENER
    The weeds which his broad-spreading leaves did shelter,

                    . . .

    Are plucked up, root and all, by Bolingbroke . . .

                                                    (III.4.50, 52)

The 1940s critic E. M. W. Tillyard saw the Gardener as a type of ideal king, who rules his microcosmic kingdom, the garden, correctly; and thus offers a salutary lesson in statesmanship to Richard.

The queen offers some observations on the Gardener's words which provide another possible level of interpretation:

QUEEN ISABEL
    Thou, old Adam's likeness, set to dress this garden,
    How dares thy harsh rude tongue sound this unpleasing
            news?
    What Eve, what serpent hath suggested thee
    To make a second Fall of cursèd man?

                                                    (III.4.73–6)

Here the garden becomes symbolic of Paradise, and Richard's fall is a re-enactment of the Fall of Man. This paradisal imagery shifts the symbolic associations to a different plane: the Gardener has been talking in down-to-earth and practical terms about gardening / government as a craft, a job of work, which can be done badly or well. Richard has made a mess of things, Bolingbroke is proving a better gardener. But the queen's allusions to Adam, the garden of Eden and the serpent invoke another dimension of emblematic meaning, where Richard has occupied the garden / kingdom by divine appointment, and where his deposition is a huge universal tragedy comparable to the Fall of Man.

Many critics have assumed that this scene endorses the metaphysical and theological understanding of the state, which was a powerful ideology of Shakespeare's time, and which he may for all we know have believed in. The king rules by divine right; to depose him is a universal crime that must have been 'suggested', like the temptation of man, by the powers of evil. But that is clearly not the Gardener's view at all. He expresses a much more secular understanding of politics and history, in which all the emphasis is on the necessity of hard and effective work. Kingdoms are not lost and won by the will of Providence, but by the agency of human action:

GARDENER
> King Richard he is in the mighty hold
> Of Bolingbroke. Their fortunes both are weighed.
> In your lord's scale is nothing but himself
> And some few vanities that make him light.
> But in the balance of great Bolingbroke
> Besides himself are all the English peers,
> And with that odds he weighs King Richard down.

(III.4.83–9)

If the queen's theological metaphors encourage us to think of the parallelism between king and gardener, the Gardener's pragmatic common sense suggests a much stronger contrast between courtly vanity and earnest craftsmanship. The religious overtones emanate from a character whose position embodies (whether by choice or subjection) the time-wasting idleness of courtly play ('What sport shall we devise . . .?', III.4.1); the melancholy secular understanding of history from the character who represents the gospel of work.

4. Conclusions

History

We have already discussed the striking taciturnity with which Boling-broke announces his intention to succeed Richard and become king.

BOLINGBROKE
  In God's name I'll ascend the regal throne.

(IV.1.113)

That curious and puzzling economy with words contrasts sharply with the voluminous loquacity of the next speaker, the Bishop of Carlisle, who overwhelms the verbal presence of the new 'silent king' with some thirty-five lines of powerful and prophetic argument against his succession and the deposition of Richard:

BISHOP OF CARLISLE
  What subject can give sentence on his king? –
  And who sits here that is not Richard's subject?

  . . .

  My Lord of Hereford here, whom you call king,
  Is a foul traitor to proud Hereford's King;
  And if you crown him, let me prophesy
  The blood of English shall manure the ground,
  And future ages groan for this foul act.
  Peace shall go sleep with Turks and infidels,
  And in this seat of peace tumultuous wars
  Shall kin with kin, and kind with kind, confound.
  Disorder, horror, fear, and mutiny
  Shall here inhabit, and this land be called
  The field of Golgotha and dead men's skulls.
  O, if you raise this house against this house
  It will the woefullest division prove
  That ever fell upon this cursèd earth.
  Prevent it; resist it; let it not be so,
  Lest child, child's children, cry against you woe.

(IV.1.121–2, 134–49)

The bishop has of course chosen a highly charged and sensitive moment to make his plea for the proposed deposition to be reversed. Since formally Richard is still king, and Bolingbroke has not yet assumed the sovereign power, a subject should theoretically be within his rights to defend the title of the reigning monarch and to lodge an objection against Bolingbroke's candidacy for the throne. But if in fact the real political transfer of power has already taken place, along with the fundamental and irreversible shift we have already seen in the balance of military power from Richard to Bolingbroke, and if the latter is already *de facto* if not *de jure* (in fact if not in law) absolute king, then the Bishop of Carlisle is uttering words which will obviously be taken, by the powers that be, as treasonable. He accuses Bolingbroke of being a 'foul traitor' and calls upon the nobility to 'resist' his accession. It comes therefore as no surprise when Northumberland arrests Carlisle on a charge of high treason. Northumberland is assuming, of course, that Henry is already king, since 'high' treason must relate to the sovereign. It is in the name of a king whose power is established but whose legitimate authority is not yet recognized that Northumberland arrests the Bishop, effectively gags his eloquence and swiftly removes him from any capacity for political influence.

The difference between Bolingbroke's terseness and Carlisle's eloquence parallels the contrast we have already discussed between Bolingbroke's sparsity of utterance, his willingness to let actions speak for themselves, and Richard's preference for elaborate public deployment of the powers of language. Clearly Carlisle does nothing at all to change the movement of events. If his speech of prophesy has any kind of force or power, it is of the same kind as Richard's speeches of self-sacrifice and martyrdom – the power that belongs to words, to poetry, to art and to myth. The fact that Bolingbroke, here and elsewhere in the play, can find no language with which to justify his actions in assuming the throne, while the language of those who oppose his usurpation can touch such plangent intensities of apocalyptic feeling, is perhaps the strongest argument in favour of the view that the play presents Richard's fall as a tragic martyrdom, and Bolingbroke's rise as an illegitimate and unauthorized seizure of power by the criminal opportunism of *force majeure*.

This is one of the most persuasive critical readings of *Richard II*, and undoubtedly these qualitative differences between the party of the deposed and the party of the usurper have exercised a powerful influence over critical interpretation of this play. For not only is the Bishop of Carlisle a fiery and arresting orator, he is also absolutely correct in his predictions and in his political analysis. The overthrow of the legitimate ruler certainly does lead to deep internal conflict within the nation, raising 'this house' against 'this house' – that is, provoking antagonism between parties and factions, perhaps between the 'house' of parliament and the 'house' of the monarchy. It also results in arraigning against one another those familial groupings later to be thrown into bloody conflict as the 'houses' of Lancaster and York. There is, in addition, a biblical allusion, echoing St Mark's observations on the dangers of a 'house' (that is, family, household) 'divided against itself' (*Mark.* 3.25). Civil hostilities will follow immediately, as Shakespeare showed in the next play of his historical sequence, *Henry IV, Part 1*: the coronation oil is hardly dry on Henry's forehead before Northumberland and his son Henry Percy begin to feel that the new king doesn't sufficiently acknowledge the support of those who backed his usurpation. The young Percy begins to plot resistance against the king, and ultimately finds himself fighting the king's army in pitched combat at Shrewsbury, the climactic battle of the play, and dying at the hands of Henry VI's son, Prince Hal. The full-scale civil wars of Henry VI's reign were to Shakespeare (in every sense) already a matter of historical record. As I mentioned earlier, he had already written the sequence of plays chronicling the violent internecine struggles of Lancaster and York. While the Bishop of Carlisle's predictions seem to follow as naturally as night follows day, Henry is continually planning pilgrimages and crusades that never actually happen. It is as if in his case there will always be some fundamental incompatibility between achievement and aspiration, circumstance and will, destiny and desire.

The language and imagery of Carlisle's speech connect it with much Elizabethan political thought familiar to us. From royal proclamations and homilies read in the church pulpits, to some of the most sophisticated works of political science, we can find everywhere this same set of emphases: the vital necessity of preserving and maintaining order, whatever corruptions and abuses may mar the state's majesty; the importance of fostering concord, unity and obedience within the social hierarchy and within the structure of the family; the powerful moral and religious sanctions invoked against acts of disobedience, rebellion, treachery, subversion. This ideology, however ingeniously elaborated it may appear in Elizabethan culture, was of course little more than a decorative cloaking of the interests of the state. The dominant classes of Elizabethan society – the monarchy and land-owning aristocracy – obviously had a vested interest in the preservation of social order, and in the active discouragement of any rebellious emotions of discontent and resistance.

At one time critics writing about Shakespeare's historical dramas tended to argue that this was *the* political philosophy of the Elizabethan age, that any other conception of politics was at the time more or less unthinkable, and that Shakespeare as a man of his time must have shared this dominant view. In the context of that critical tradition, the Bishop of Carlisle is actually a kind of spokesman for the author. Now this political vision may, for all we know, have been the one Shakespeare held and believed in, but to argue that it was is to make a very large and circumstantial inference from the evidence we actually have. No-one could be more anonymous and shadowy, in all but the basic details of a biography, than the figure of Shakespeare. Since the chosen medium of his art was the impersonal objectivity of the drama, we can never with any confidence say that Shakespeare thought or said so-and-so; we can only observe that such-and-such a character in such-and-such a play thought or said so-and-so. The Bishop of Carlisle's loyalist rhetoric is there in Shakespeare's play; it is part of it; but we have no evidence at all to indicate that Shakespeare in any way shared the bishop's sentiments.

The view I have just been discussing was founded and promulgated by critics such as G. Wilson Knight, E. M. W. Tillyard and J. Dover Wilson, who were all writing in the 1940s or even earlier. By the early 1950s other critics (such as Irving Ribner and A. P. Rossiter) were already beginning to question the arguments of the Tillyard school. They were not so much concerned to challenge the notion of a dominant, conservative Elizabethan ideology, but they could not accept that so unique and incomparable a genius as Shakespeare could have believed what every stupid Elizabethan peasant believed. It began to be argued that Shakespeare's own political vision, in so far as it could be inferred from the plays, was far more idiosyncratic and independent of common beliefs and dominant ideologies than the Tillyard school had asserted.

The next stage in the development of this critical tradition, which happened in the 1960s and 1970s, was a revaluation of this conservative model of Elizabethan culture and ideology – Tillyard's 'Elizabethan world-picture'. Critics (such as Moody Prior and Henry A. Kelly) began to recognize the standard Bishop-of-Carlisle-orthodoxy as representative of the most entrenched and backward-looking elements of Elizabethan thought, harking right back to the Christian providentialism of the Middle Ages. In fact Elizabethan culture was in Shakespeare's time being strongly influenced by new ideas: humanistic ethics and philosophy, scientific discoveries and explorations, and the advanced political and historiographical thought of Italy. These progressive currents of Renaissance thought were beginning to propose that man was more central to the world than God, and that the organization of societies, and the laws of development which operated in history, could be seen in terms of human agency rather than as an unfolding of divine Providence. In this body of critical interpretation, Shakespeare becomes either a disciple of Machiavelli, or a sceptical observer dramatizing conflicts between old and new ideas – between the Bishop of Carlisle's orthodoxy and Bolingbroke's political machiavellianism – in a transitional moment of his national history.

There is much to be said for the latter framework of interpretation. It seems to me, however, to suffer from certain theoretical weaknesses. The sceptical Elizabethan observer of Renaissance history is too often a stand-in for the twentieth-century intellectual, resigned and uncommitted, interested in everything, believing in nothing. Critics who have acknowledged the importance of the influence on Elizabethan culture of Italian humanistic ideas, have sometimes drawn from that body of thought a kind of universalizing cynicism in which all political action and belief, in whatever time or place, become much the same: opportunism, manipulation, corruption, the oppression of the weak by the strong and the simple by the clever. The assimilation of Shakespeare's plays to that kind of generalizing, universalizing philosophy results in a significant loss of historical substance, a significant simplification of those thoughtful, imaginative and historically informed constructions of historical narrative that we find in the actual plays themselves.

I started with the point that Bolingbroke has no justifying language with which to challenge Carlisle's denunciation. His only means of negotiating such a challenge is that of silencing the speaker. We should not forget, on the other hand, that Bolingbroke and the other barons have up to this point in the action been perfectly able to command a definite political language of their own. That aristocratic discourse can display its own kinds of intensity when articulating matters of chivalry and revenge, honour and justice. But when applied to the more centrally 'constitutional' matters of royal authority and sovereign power, the baronial language certainly sounds thinly rationalistic and solidly pragmatic by contrast with the vividly imaginative poetry of prophesy and martyrdom employed by Richard and the Bishop of Carlisle. None the less it is a perfectly valid political language, embodying definite principles and intelligible values – respect for the rule of law, the rights of property, the obligations of the state and the privileges of the aristocratic subject. The feudal language spoken by Bolingbroke and the other barons is obviously an attempt on the part of the historical playwright to dramatize the historical specificity of political experience, in an age when men and women thought and felt differently from their modern Elizabethan counterparts. It is precisely at the point where the baron finds himself king that that feudal discourse of contract and fealty, legal rights and royal obligations, breaks down and has nothing effective to say. The chaotic comedy of the earlier part of the same scene – Bolingbroke's inquiry into the circumstances of Gloucester's death, where gloves and chivalric challenges fly around the room with bewildering multiplicity (Aumerle challenges so many people that he runs out of gloves and has to ask if he can borrow one from somebody) – gives some indication of the inadequacy of the feudal perspective as a basis for government.

Once Henry is king he has to stop thinking and acting like a rebellious baron, and start thinking and acting like a king. He never succeeds, in Shakespeare's dramatization of his reign, in reconciling the contradictions between his feudal and his monarchical ideologies. In a fascinating speech in *Henry IV, Part 1* (III.2) the king holds up as a role-model to his own son, Prince Hal – who spends all his time in taverns and appears to be a 'truant to chivalry' – the example of Henry Percy. If Hal were more like Percy, he would appear to be a more convincing candidate for the throne. What distinguishes young Percy, and commands the king's admiration, is the fact that he is successfully leading an armed rebellion against the power of Henry himself; Percy is showing himself capable of the political and military exploits which brought Henry himself to power. A man proves his qualifications for kingship by being able to overthrow another king. It is a dangerous idea for a king to believe, and one which poisons his relationship with his own son. The prince can earn his father's respect only by showing himself capable of rebellion and usurpation. Towards the end of Shakespeare's *Henry IV, Part 2*, during the king's terminal illness, the prince believes him to be dead, and takes the crown from his pillow. King Henry wakes to find the crown he seized from Richard prematurely taken from him by his own son.

Richard II, then, is a play informed by a very modern sense of history. When Shakespeare looked back at the events of the fourteenth and fifteenth centuries, he did not see men and women thinking and feeling in much the same ways as those who surrounded him in contemporary England. He saw people thinking and feeling within the framework of certain historical ideologies. Shakespeare's history plays are not simple reflections of the time in which they were written, 'mirrors of Elizabethan policy': they involve the active exercise of a historical imagination, capable of recognizing the differences between the present and the past. The conflict between Richard and Bolingbroke is not dramatized only within a framework of Elizabethan ideas and assumptions; nor is it depicted as a struggle between an ancient ideology of medieval kingship and a new political realism. The play is an act of historiography which dramatizes and interprets a significant moment of historical transition in a society of the past.

Politics

I seem to have been arguing that *Richard II* should be understood purely as a historical play, and implying that it had no contemporary significance, nothing to say about its own time at all. It would clearly be wrong to assert such an argument of any form of cultural production, and I must now offer some observations to redress that imbalance. A good starting point for an assessment of an Elizabethan play's contemporary significance is to look at the nature of the theatre in which it would initially have been produced.

The type of theatre in which *Richard II* would have been produced was the Elizabethan public playhouse, the open-air amphitheatre with its big, bare stage, and its audience crowded around in the yard or seated in the galleries. Our standard image for that theatre is the famous Globe: *Richard II* was probably produced in one of the earlier buildings, such as the Swan. We are familiar, from modern performances of the history plays, with the convention of dressing actors in costumes appropriate to the historical period of the play's action; in this case, the late fourteenth century. Historical costume actually came into the drama quite late, towards the end of the eighteenth and the beginning of the nineteenth centuries. In the Elizabethan theatre and later, plays were performed in what we now call 'modern dress', the ordinary contemporary fashion of the period.

The resources of Shakespeare's theatre would not then seem to have offered much in the way of visual and spatial representation for a historical period of the past. A modern film like Olivier's *Henry V* (1944) can mock up a convincing simulation of history and give us a battle-field inhabited by actors in fifteenth-century armour, weapons, horses, castles and all the material trappings of a late-medieval society. But a stage without historical scenery or historical costume would not seem to be particularly well equipped to represent history. It would perhaps be more natural to assume that, like our own 'modern-dress' productions, these plays in performance would be interpreted as pointing to the present time of their production rather than the past time of their historical subject.

The one thing we are forgetting here is the play's language. Although the other elements of a stage performance have a profound and decisive influence on the communicative medium of the drama, the character of the Elizabethan theatre inevitably focused particularly strong attention on the actors and on the language they spoke. The actor who played Richard may have appeared on stage looking much like a sixteenth-century king, but the language he spoke would have transported him directly back into the fourteenth century:

KING RICHARD
> Marshal, ask yonder knight in arms
> Both who he is, and why he cometh hither
> Thus plated in habiliments of war . . .

(I.3.26–8)

In the Elizabethan court such language of chivalry could only be spoken in the context of a courtly game, in which history had been transformed into romance. The actor playing Richard on the stage of the Swan theatre would be positioning himself by his physical appearance in present time, but declaring himself verbally as a figure from the remote past.

That sense of a degree of tension between separate elements of the dramatic medium gives us an indication as to how 'history' would have been represented on the Elizabethan stage. If there is a contradiction between a character's appearance and the language he speaks, then the drama could not in that kind of theatre have been functioning 'realistically'. 'Naturalism', the kind of dramatic convention that aims at a convincing representation of psychological and social reality on stage, only appeared in the nineteenth century. In our modern theatres we can find both realistic and non-realistic ways of producing drama. In film and television drama we are accustomed to overwhelmingly naturalistic methods of performance, based on psychological verisimilitude and location filming. But in the Elizabethan period, and for centuries afterwards, the drama was not naturalistic; audiences did not expect to see convincing representations of real human experiences in an accurately depicted social environment. In a play like *Richard II* characters like the Gardener, who resembles figures from an allegorical pageant or masque rather than being a plausible characterization, could appear with no sense of incongruity; soliloquies would be spoken directly to the audience, thus disrupting any movement towards naturalistic representation; and the whole atmosphere of a daylight performance – with a visible audience, no scenery, minimal props, no lighting, contemporary costume – would have worked against the establishing of any serious degree of dramatic illusion.

Since the drama was produced and received more as a conventionalized ritual performance than as a believable slice of life, its capacity for signification, for making meanings possible, would not have been restricted or pinned down to any one dimension. There is no reason at all why a play like *Richard II* could not have been understood to signify meanings for the present and for the past simultaneously. The unlocalized stage of the Elizabethan theatre allowed for great flexibility of time and space; many of Shakespeare's plays rove across continents and cover immense gaps of time, without ever departing from the bare boards of the stage. Neoclassical critics of the popular stage like Sir Philip Sidney objected to this theatrical liberty. They believed that a play should preserve the 'unities' laid down by Aristotle, confining itself to a single day, a single place and a single action. To Sidney it was ridiculous that a stage should be supposed to represent Asia on one side, and Africa on the other. If we accept that possibility of flexible signification, then there is no reason at all why the fourteenth and sixteenth centuries should not meet on the same stage. At the same time, the fact that Africa and Asia were simultaneously represented does not mean that the audience would confuse them: they remained quite distinct places. Because the stage could look like anywhere, and represent everywhere, that does not mean it was taken to be nowhere. Shakespeare's *Antony and Cleopatra* moves its focus continually from Rome to Egypt: the stage always looked the same, but only by completely ignoring the play's language could a spectator confuse or fail to recognize the difference between the two empires. A historical play on the Elizabethan stage was a complex montage capable of connecting and distinguishing very diverse realities, past and present time, near and remote space. Though the medium juxtaposed such disparate realities, it didn't simply blur them indistinguishably into an incoherent mass of 'universal human experience'. It could link and separate, connect and distinguish, compare and contrast, and secure a complex knowledge of history through a vigorous interplay of similarity and difference.

With these observations in mind, we can return to the evidence I mentioned in the Introduction, which demonstrates that *Richard II* must have been considered a politically significant and perhaps politically dangerous play in its own time. First there is the evidence of censorship. The early printed Quarto texts of the play, three of them issued in 1597 and 1598, all omit the central section of IV.1, lines 154–317, which show Richard handing over his crown to Bolingbroke. This passage was restored in the fourth Quarto text, published in 1608. What the printed texts do not tell us, of course, is whether or not that passage was also omitted in stage performances. The censorship of a section of the deposition-scene in print alone, however, tells us two things: that the play could be read, at least by a censor, as having some reference to the Elizabethan present day; and that the spectacle of a monarch voluntarily handing over the crown was considered by Elizabeth's Master of the Revels to be too dangerous an action for representation on stage. The censor's nervousness can be linked historically to anxieties about the succession, which were not resolved until shortly before Elizabeth's death. Since the deposition was restored in 1608, the significance attributed to it seems to have consisted in some possible allusion to Elizabeth: her death in 1603 evidently cleared the way for the dangerous matter to be published.

On 8 February 1601 the Earl of Essex embarked on his abortive rebellion, which ended for him in failure and execution for treason. On the previous day some of Essex's supporters persuaded Shakespeare's acting company, the Lord Chamberlain's Men, to stage a play about the deposition and death of Richard II at the Globe theatre. The actors were offered a fee of forty shillings. Since Shakespeare was that company's resident writer, it is most likely that this was his play. The actors later admitted to some reluctance, since they thought they would get few spectators at a performance of such an old and unfamiliar play, but in deference to their client's request it was produced. Perhaps they were nervous about more than audience figures. The details of this incident were preserved in the records of Essex's trial, so it is obvious that the players could have been in serious trouble. In the event, they were cleared.

The only possible reason Essex's men could have had for commissioning this performance of an old play is political. They must have hoped that a re-enactment of the deposition of Richard by Bolingbroke would symbolically establish Essex in the justice of his cause, and perhaps inspire the people to support him. Evidently Essex wanted to encourage a systematic historical identification of Elizabeth with Richard, and of himself with Bolingbroke. His patronage of this play parallels his covert support for a historical study by Sir John Hayward, which featured a dedication to Essex, hinting at the same comparison. It is evident from these details that *Richard II* was in its own time available for a subversive reading: for an interpretation which characterized Richard (and by implication Elizabeth) as an unpopular ruler, and cast Bolingbroke (and by implication Essex) in the light of the country's saviour.

Although Shakespeare had acquaintances in common with Essex, such as the Earl of Southampton, and may well have moved on the edges of that quite extensive circle of progressive intellectuals who gathered around the earl, few people have seriously argued that *Richard II* was originally written with such a political intention in mind. In the political mythology of the age, the parallels between Elizabeth and Richard, Essex and Bolingbroke, were current; a play about *Richard II* fitted naturally into them. It is not impossible that Shakespeare had closer connections with the Essex party, but the evidence is not strong enough to justify more than a guess.

On the other hand, it would be misleading to suggest that the play was purely an innocent object of opportunistic exploitation. *Richard II* goes further than drawing a simple opposition between medieval providentialism and secular humanism, between the divine right of kings and a constitutional theory of the rights of the subject. The play certainly represents the belief in metaphysical sovereignty. But it also demonstrates the socio-cultural process by which that belief is made: it takes an idea, and shows it to be (what in modern terms we would call) an ideology. The construction of Richard's personal myth, together with the circumstances of his fall and of Bolingbroke's rise, are all shown taking place within a historical process that seems to proceed by secular laws of historical development, rather than by the management of divine Providence. That difference of perspective on history may seem to us fairly academic and theoretical, but it counted for a great deal in Shakespeare's own time. If history was not the gradual unfolding of the will of God, but the activity of man pursuing his aims, then society was revealed to be a social contract, dependent for its survival on the consent of the subject as well as the power of the ruler. Kings were exposed as vulnerable to deposition and political dismissal, and a disaffected aristocrat like the Earl of Essex could seriously contemplate the prospect of taking his destiny into his own hands and attempting by the assertion of human will to change the world.

Tragedy

I have attempted to define the nature of *Richard II*'s historical vision, and to give some indication of how we may begin to consider it as a play about sixteenth-century politics. The Elizabethans also called the play a 'tragical history', and it clearly has features which relate it to the genre of tragedy. It remains then to make some suggestions as to how *Richard II* may be addressed as an Elizabethan tragedy.

Writing about tragedy in the context of Renaissance drama is an undertaking fraught with difficulties. When the Elizabethans themselves tried to theorize about tragedy they drew their ideas from Aristotle, and many subsequent critics have tried to fit Shakespearean tragedy into the Aristotelian mould. It is quite evident, however, that just as the Eliza-bethan drama was composed with scant attention to the rules of classical dramatic theory (for example, the 'unities'), so Elizabethan tragedy paid little heed to Aristotle's notions (for example, 'catharsis'), drawing rather on examples of dramatic practice such as the plays of Seneca. Reading Sir Philip Sidney's observations on tragedy in his *Defence of Poetry*, which lean heavily on Aristotle, it is difficult not to feel that the critic's theoretical perspective is quite out of step with current dramatic practice. The great theories of tragedy – those of Hegel, Nietzsche and Bradley – seem to have been constructed at other historical times; though they can offer some useful means of access to Elizabethan tragedy, they do not offer any comprehensive tragic theory into which the Elizabethan drama can be located.

In some ways *Richard II* invites comparison with the very crude, simple and popular conception of tragedy held in the Middle Ages, before the humanistic revival of the Renaissance put classical culture immovably on the agenda. For Chaucer a tragedy was simply a kind of story, a particular structure of narrative, which always followed the same pattern, and which taught a simple moral lesson. Tragedy told the tale of an historical or legendary character, who began by occupying a position of worldly greatness, wealth, or power, and who by chance, accident or misfortune fell from that elevated position into humility, poverty and misery. The nature of the tale inculcated a simple moral: none of the benefits of this world are to be trusted; fortune may bestow temporary rewards, but these can be torn away in a moment's unexpected reversal; men should be encouraged to recognize the instability and vicissitude of mortal life and urged to trust only in the immortality of heaven. Chaucer's 'Monk's Tale' in the *Canter-bury Tales* is a good example of how medieval thinkers conceived of tragedy. The 'Monk's Tale' is a series of short summaries of exemplary doomed lives from history, scripture and legend, all strung together by the simple Christian doctrine that taught the transience of worldly goods, the instability of earthly power. The immensely popular Tudor poem *The Mirror for Magistrates* (1587) used precisely the same form. King Richard II appears in the course of its gloomy sequence of instructively fated destinies, confessing the folly of living and ruling by 'blind lust'. Other exemplary figures of tragic experience in the same compilation are Thomas of Woodstock, Thomas Mowbray and Henry Percy.

Richard's language is full of the imagery and emotion of medieval tragedy.

RICHARD

> Join not with grief, fair woman, do not so,
> To make my end too sudden. Learn, good soul,
> To think our former state a happy dream,
> From which awaked the truth of what we are
> Shows us but this. I am sworn brother, sweet,
> To grim Necessity . . .

(V.1.16–21)

Waking from the illusory dream by means of which men place their trust in worldly power and happiness, the tragic figure discovers his true subjection to 'Necessity'. In that discovery lies the possibility of a sad and resigned wisdom: 'the truth of what we are'.

Now of course *Richard II* is nothing like as simple as this type of crude Christian propaganda – the medieval tragedy – though it certainly has more in common with such works than it has with Aristotle's *Poetics*. Richard's fall from power clearly represents an exemplary story of fate's uncertainties, and his suffering and self-discovery are basic ingredients of tragedy. But there is no simple, easily intelligible message to be derived from Shakespeare's dramatization, as there is from each of the tragic narratives contained in Chaucer's *Monk's Tale*. Nor would we derive much assistance, except of the most general kind, from other theories of tragedy. Richard's fall doesn't seem to offer us the mandatory resolution of pity and fear by catharsis which for Aristotle constituted the essential tragic experience; he is scarcely the great self-destructive tragic hero of Nietzsche's theory; and we would be hard pressed to abstract from his character any weakness as singular and isolable as Bradley's 'tragic flaw'.

A more accessible question would be to ask what kinds of attention are likely to be given to the play if it is interpreted as a tragedy rather than a historical or political drama. What meanings does the play-text deliver if a reading is focused on the tragic dimension? To start with, a preoccupation with tragic suffering and self-revelation will tend to isolate the figure of Richard from the other elements of the drama. The tragic hero towers in significance over every other character, and rather than seeming a part of the play's world, offers to incorporate the representative experiences of the world into his own person.

Here is an example of the type of interpretation likely to emerge from such a preoccupation with Richard as the transcendent tragic colossus of the play:

The play, although it touches upon this subject, is not about a struggle for power between two royal houses, nor even between two royal men, despite contrasts in politics and temperament. Shakespeare could have written a play of political intrigue, and made the military action which accompanies it a good deal more uncertain and exciting – the material was there in Holinshed. Instead, he placed the emphasis on Richard's nature and behaviour, and gave his play the order and unity of biography.

> (Peter Ure, *The Arden Shakespeare: Richard II*, p. lxiii)

In terms of this interpretation the first two acts of the play are little more than a preface to the drama of individual tragic suffering that begins in Act III. Peter Ure continues (p. lxix):

... that part of his fall which was political and entailed the loss of power had been accomplished; there remains that aspect of it which trenches upon a sacred tragedy, the divesting of royalty of its mysterious panoply.... Shakespeare bundled the narrative of causes away into the first two and a half acts so that he might more fully set forth the drama of the sufferer constrained to reduce himself from king to man by shedding the 'great glory' of the Name.

It should be quite obvious here that the play is being badly distorted and misrepresented in the interests of a single important emphasis. It is perfectly true that Richard's suffering becomes dominant in the second half of the play, but if its first half is nothing more than a crude throwing together of merely circumstantial and 'political' causes into a haphazard 'bundle', then we must begin to wonder just what kind of half-baked dramatic structure we are dealing with.

Apart from the fact that Richard's tragedy is always, as I have argued at length in the preceding pages, inextricably involved with the political and historical circumstances within which it is dramatized and located, such a view takes no account at all of the complementary role of Bolingbroke. For Bolingbroke does not simply provide a narrative of success to contradict Richard's tale of tragic loss and subjection. The tragic destiny that dogs Richard seems to cling ominously around Henry as soon as he becomes king. Richard's great speeches of tragic poetry in III.2 propose that the tragic destiny is inseparable from the possession of power; he may stand here alone and isolated in the magnitude of his suffering, but he can see quite clearly that his successor's ascent to greatness will be hollowed and haunted by exactly the same tragic fate. Shakespeare seems to be dramatizing here something more in the order of a tragic society, a tragic historical period, than the individual tragedy of a hero isolated by the intensity of his fate.

Raymond Williams, in an important modern treatment of the theory of tragedy, argues that historically tragedy has gradually shifted its focus, with an inexorable development, downwards in the social scale. Early tragedy always dwelt on the suffering of a great king, or even a god; Renaissance tragedy either followed Greek drama and enacted the tragedy of a king, or focused more on the tragedies of those slightly below the rank of monarch, though still major figures in the state – the prince, the general, the warlord; in the nineteenth century the tragic hero (and in an important development, the tragic heroine) would be a symbolic representative of the bourgeois family; and in the twentieth century it became possible to dramatize tragedies of working-class life. *Richard II* is in many ways an antique tragic structure, dramatizing the rise and fall, the pride and the humiliation of a great king. But because Shakespeare seems to have been moving towards that more secular and sociological conception of history that I have described, and that the play seems to me to represent, its focus spreads around and beyond the individual tragic hero, and begins to acknowledge the possibility of a society rendered tragic by the political and historical contradictions that lay at its heart.

Further Reading

I have used as my basic text the New Penguin Shakespeare *Richard II*, ed. Stanley Wells (Harmondsworth, Penguin, 1969). Another useful text is the New Cambridge Shakespeare edition, ed. Andrew Gurr (Cambridge, Cambridge University Press, 1984), which combines the usual explanatory footnotes and references with a sensible, readable introduction that pays some attention to the history of *Richard II* in the theatre. The Arden Shakespeare edition, ed. Peter Ure (London, Methuen, 5th edition, 1961), has an elaborate scholarly apparatus, but seems now decidedly old-fashioned in its basic critical and theoretical approach.

The initial foundations of a genuinely historical criticism of plays like *Richard II* were laid by books like E. M. W. Tillyard's *Shakespeare's History Plays* (London, Chatto & Windus, 1944); Lily B. Campbell's *Shakespeare's Histories: Mirrors of Elizabethan Policy* (San Marino, California, Huntington Library, 1947); and Derek Traversi's *Shakespeare: from 'Richard II' to 'Henry V'* (London, Hollis & Carter, 1957). The conservatism of their approach, with its characterization of Shakespeare as an orthodox conformist, was questioned by Irving Ribner, *The English History Play in the Age of Shakespeare* (Princeton, N.J., Princeton University Press, 1957). The Tillyardian characterization of Shakespeare as a medieval rather than a Renaissance thinker was challenged by Moody E. Prior, *The Drama of Power* (Evanston, Illinois, Northwestern University Press, 1973) and by Wilbur Sanders, *The Dramatist and the Received Idea* (Cambridge, Cambridge University Press, 1968), which demonstrated the influence of progressive Renaissance ideas on Shakespeare's history plays. Henry A. Kelly, in *Divine Providence in the England of Shakespeare's Histories* (Cambridge, Mass., Harvard University Press, 1970), showed the variety and complexity of historiographical thought in Shakespeare's time and in his historical plays. Graham Holderness in *Shakespeare's History* (Dublin, Gill & Macmillan, 1985) examined imaginative developments in the historical drama alongside developments in the theoretical construction of history.

Texts of the play usually print extracts from the important sources, such as Holinshed's *The Chronicles of England, Scotland and Ireland* (1577, second edition 1587) and Daniel's *The First Four Books of the Civil Wars between the Two Houses of Lancaster and York* (1595), which are not very accessible in themselves (though very rewarding to read), and also refer to other definite or possible sources. Geoffrey Bullough's *Narrative and Dramatic Sources of Shakespeare* (London, Routledge & Kegan Paul, vol. 3, 1960) compiles a comprehensive collection of extracts from sources. Graham Holderness discusses the range and variety of *Richard II*'s sources, and the historical background of the opening trial, in Graham Holderness, John Turner and Nick Potter, *Shakespeare: The Play of History* (London, Macmillan, 1988). A fuller treatment of the legal background can be found in Edna Boris Zwick, *Shakespeare's English Kings, the People and the Law* (New Jersey, Associated University Presses, 1978).